THE Big Book OF Personality Tests

90 EASY-TO-SCORE QUIZZES
THAT REVEAL THE REAL YOU

SALVATORE V. DIDATO, PH.D.

BLACK DOG
& LEVENTHAL
PUBLISHERS
NEW YORK

Published by

Black Dog & Leventhal Publishers, Inc.
151 West 19th Street
New York, NY 10011

Distributed by

Workman Publishing Company
708 Broadway
New York, NY 10003

Front cover design by Cindy LaBreacht

Back cover design by Tony Meisel

Interior design by Martin Lubin

Cartoons reprinted with permission of *The Saturday Evening Post*, BFL&MS, Inc.

Manufactured in China

ISBN: 1-57912-281-7

h g f

Library of Congress Cataloging-in-Publication Data
Didato, Salvatore V.
 The big book of personality tests : 100 easy-to-score quizzes that
reveal the real you / Salvatore V. Didato.
     p. cm.
 ISBN 1-57912-281-7
 1. Personality tests. I. Title.
BF698.5.D53 2003
155.2'83--dc21
                                        2003000315

Acknowledgements

I would like to thank my wife, Dr. Paulette Didato, for her assistance in editing and proofreading this book; and my son, David Didato, for his valuable help in the technical computer adjustments required to prepare effective copy.

Also, I wish to thank authors Wayne Dyer and Evan Hunter (a.k.a. Ed McBain) for their sound advice about the finer points of book publishing; and Walter Anderson, CEO of Parade Publications, for his encouragement in pursuing the quiz as a format to convey psychological understanding.

I especially wish to honor the memory of the late Dr. Norman Vincent Peale, who over the years provided this writer with incomparable insights into the human condition.

SALVATORE V. DIDATO, PH.D.

Contents

Introduction

Welcome to your personal quiz book! With some 3,000 personality tests in use today, we are certainly the most analyzed creatures on earth. We are also among the most self-conscious. We never tire of putting our abilities to the test—whether it be at a simple game of Monopoly or poker or whether it's trivia on every conceivable subject from animal life to zodiac signs.

The one topic that commands our overwhelming attention is our self. Anything that sheds light on the fascinating mystery of our emotions—why we feel and behave as we do, why we do what we shouldn't and don't do what we should—compels our interest. We revel in knowing what makes us tick.

And although the sages of old have intoned, "know thyself," in this hectic, non-contemplative society, with its many distractions from our inner selves, self-knowledge is perhaps the most difficult of all tasks to achieve. Still, our search hasn't diminished one mite. We're ever attuned to how we compare to others, always eager to steal a glimpse of who we are, why we feel and act as we do and, more importantly, what we might become if given the opportunity.

Quizzes have been known to be great party starters. They can stimulate discussion at the dinner table, at a picnic, beach outing, or cocktail party. They are capable of raising an eyebrow over a controversial point or two or smashing a sacred cow we've nurtured all our life.

HOW TO GET THE MOST OUT OF THIS BOOK

In planning this book, I felt that the quiz format would be an interesting and entertaining way to impart understanding on a wide range of human psychology subjects. The tests are drawn from the research studies, surveys, and clinical experience of some of the finest minds in social science, psychology, and psychiatry.

Although everything is open to interpretation and these tests are therefore not foolproof or the final word, I am confident that they do have more scientific credibility than the average quiz in the daily tabloids. Indeed, many of the questions in this book might very well be those that a professional psychologist would ask during an evaluation. For example, some of the following items would be pivotal to any psychological profiler:

- ✔ Do you agree that a child should be told up front what the discipline will be if he or she steps out of line? (See "Are You Parent Perfect?" on page 66)

- ✔ Would you like to be hypnotized? (See "Are You an Undiscovered Creative Genius?" page 152)

- ✔ Do you have difficulty accepting compliments about your accomplishments? (See "Do You Fear Success?" page 138)

- ✔ Do you like to gamble on football games, lotteries, or races, or to play games of chance? (See "How Ambitious Are You? page 102)

✔ Do you believe it's okay to tell a white lie in order to avoid hassles? (See "Are You a Con Artist in Disguise?" page 80)

✔ Are you able to accept compliments without feeling uneasy? (See "How High Is Your Self-Esteem?" page 184)

✔ Do you often engage in "taboo" activities, or wish you did? (See "Could You Break the Law?" page 86)

TEST THE TESTS FOR FUN

To verify any given test's conclusions, try to rate yourself on the particular trait being tested before you begin. For added interest, ask a friend to join you in your self-ratings, then compare answers. But please be aware that if you disagree with your score, it might mean that either you slanted your responses (unintentionally or not) or that you may not have an accurate view of yourself. If this happens, go back and review your answers. Considering how you might have responded differently often provides insights that will help you pinpoint your answers the next time around.

TO THINE OWN SELF BE TRUE

Will this book really give you a window onto your true self? A lot depends on you. To get the most from a quiz, don't fudge your answers. No one's peering over your shoulder, so be straightforward. Usually it's best to respond without too much deliberation. And though it's tempting, try not to minimize weaknesses or maximize strengths. If you're honest and accurate in your answers, you should come away with a fairly realistic picture of yourself as you really are.

Enjoy the tests!

SALVATORE V. DIDATO, PH.D.

CHAPTER 1

The Real You

"'Because it is here'—that's all I can get out of him."

How Daring Are You?

Though they may not be daredevils in the strictest sense of the word, some people enjoy the public image associated with being adventurous. When we think of such types, certain characters come to mind, like Mario Andretti, speed car racer; Sir Richard Branson, Virgin Group C.E.O. and hot air balloonist; and Robby Knievel, stunt motorcyclist. Studies show that daring persons often have more self-confidence and higher IQ levels than those who are more reluctant. But this is only part of the picture.

At the Institute of Psychiatry at the University of London, H. J. Eysenck and S. G. Eysenck performed extensive research on adventuresome people. In their sample of 1,200 subjects they found that daredevils are more extraverted and impulsive on average, but that contrary to popular belief, their risk-taking is not necessarily a sign of a neurotic personality. The psychologists concluded that about one-half to two-thirds of our capacity for derring-do is probably inherited.

TEST

How much of an Andretti or Knievel are you? The following quiz lists items similar to those presented by the Eysencks. Respond "True" or "False" to the items below to determine how daring you are.

1. When shopping, I usually stick to brands I am familiar with.
True   False

2. It upsets me when one of my friends is upset.
True   False

3. Unhappy people who feel sorry for themselves irritate me.
True   False

4. It is silly for people to cry out of happiness.
True   False

5. Many animal lovers are too concerned about the comfort and feelings of animals.
True   False

6. I feel better after having a few cocktails.
True   False

7. I would probably feel sympathetic to a stranger in a group.
True   False

8. Public displays of affection annoy me somewhat.
True   False

9. I would prefer a job that required travel and change to one that kept me at home most of the time.
True   False

10. I save money regularly.
True   False

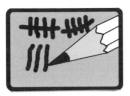

SCORING

To tally your score, give yourself 1 point for each response that matches yours.

1. *False* **2.** *False* **3.** *True* **4.** *True* **5.** *True* **6.** *True* **7.** *False* **8.** *True*
9. *True* **10.** *False*

An average score on adventurousness falls between 4 and 6.

EXPLANATION

The Eysencks found that men tend to be more adventure-seeking than women. Daring types have a strong need for variety and change in their everyday activities. Their capacity for excitement is above average, and for them, boredom is a recurring problem.

Adventurous people shy away from public displays of affection or other emotions and tend to be uncomfortable with the open expression of feelings by others. They are somewhat thick-skinned, and generally prefer to act rather than emote.

The daring among us are generally impatient for movement and gravitate toward those who seek novelty and are willing to take risks to achieve it. Strangely though, activities that the average person might deem risky, such as mountain climbing or sky diving, are often viewed by daredevils as relatively benign.

How bold or adventurous we are can vary with our social surroundings. Studies of group dynamics confirm that a pattern called "risky shift" occurs when members bolster each other's daring and shift to more risk taking than when they are alone. When committees form to decide an issue, for example, members may take more extreme stands because they are shielded by peer support. Social psychologist I. L. Janis calls this phenomenon "groupthink." In his book, *Victims of Groupthink,* he gives a telling example of how groupthink functions, citing the United States strategy committee's ill-conceived decision to invade Cambodia during the Vietnam War.

There are always extremes on the human continuum. Biochemists have dubbed strongly adventurous types "adrenaline junkies," because they seem to have a physical need to maintain high adrenaline levels in order to feel satisfaction. But as much as these outer bounds of the human psyche are influenced by psychological factors, family forces also play a crucial role in determining how daring one will be. The pulls of nature and nurture make it difficult to discern which, if either or both, is responsible for risky behavior. Studies show that parents who provide stimulating environments for their kids are likely to be adventuresome types themselves. But, if the children turn out the same way, it is tough to tell which was more influential, their inherited traits or their upbringing.

Are You Ruled by Your Mood?

Before you read on, circle what you believe most accurately describes your present mood:

Gloomy   Neutral   Happy

We all experience mood swings. Dr. Joan Oliver, in studies at St. Louis University, found that seven to ten college students out of every 100 suffer from substantial bouts of depression. This finding is consistent with those at other colleges as well.

We don't really know what causes mood swings. Some experts believe the cause is hormonal and not related to our surroundings. But to say that we're victimized by our glands is to disregard the social context in which we live. More often than not, it is people who influence our moods and it is caring people who restore us to an even keel.

TEST

Can you detect your mood at any given moment? Try the test below, which is based on Professor Oliver's research. Circle all the words that describe your feelings right now, then read on for scores and an explanation.

COLUMN 1	COLUMN 2	COLUMN 3	COLUMN 4
Humorous	Fine	Mad	Frustrated
Calm	On Top	Old	Tormented
Alive	Lucky	Tired	Unlucky
Friendly	Together	Restless	Angry
Content	Attractive	Meek	Offended
Happy	Secure	Blue	Put Down
Stable	Amused	Weak	Guilty
Rested	Brave	Lost	Irritated
Peaceful	Hopeful	Shy	Unsociable
Strong	Adaptable	Sensitive	Jumpy
Confident	Clearheaded	Cynical	Distractible
Joyful	Capable	Dull	Careless

SCORING

Columns 1 and 2 contain words associated with positive moods. The words in columns 3 and 4 connote negative moods. To tally your score, give yourself 1 point for each item circled in columns 1 and 2; subtract 1 point for each item in columns 3 and 4.

A score of 6 or more: Your current mood is highly tranquil and contented.

A score of 3 to 5: You are in an average, fairly neutral mood.

A score of negative 2 to 2: Your mood is borderline. You are susceptible to either an upswing or downswing should you have an unexpected experience.

A score of negative 5 to negative 3: You are in a low mood, but a few good times will probably pull you out of it fairly quickly.

A score of negative 6 or less: You're suffering from a strongly low mood—a "blue funk." If possible, avoid making important decisions until you feel a bit better. If this feeling has persisted for more than two months, you'd probably benefit from professional counseling.

EXPLANATION

Were you able to predict your mood? People tend to vary in their mood awareness. Those who can recognize their emotional state at any given time are usually in the best position to alter it for the better. A person with frequently changing moods is likely to be more emotionally unstable than someone whose moods are even.

We usually go through mood cycles that last between three and nine weeks. These sentimental states can vary with the day of the week and the hour of the day, as well as with the seasons. Most of us have "up" moods on Fridays and "down" moods on Mondays when we have to return to work or school. Students feel lower in spirit during the first and last half hours of the day.

If you are in a low mood, try to correct it by talking with a friend or engaging in an activity that requires a change of scenery. The blues have a way of incubating themselves, so take action as soon as possible.

How Well Do You Know Yourself?

The following quiz relates to personal attitudes and habits of behavior. It will provide self-understanding, but with a special twist depending on how you view the purpose of the test. Lest we prematurely reveal that purpose, skip ahead to the test now. An explanation follows.

TEST

Respond "True" or "False" to the items below. Don't dwell too long on the questions—give the first answer that springs to mind.

1. If it served my purposes, I would try to bluff my way past a doorman or guard.
True   False

2. I would never cut into a waiting line.
True   False

3. If I could slip into a movie without being noticed, I probably would do it.
True   False

4. I sometimes try to get even with those who have offended me.
True   False

5. If a waiter didn't charge me for an item, I probably wouldn't tell him about it.
True   False

6. I wouldn't think of having someone take the blame for my wrongdoings.
True   False

7. If I'm ignorant about something, I will admit it.
True   False

8. I try to be honest in every situation.
True   False

9. I truly don't believe that I am as prejudiced as the average person.
True   False

10. My table manners at home are as good as they are at a restaurant.
True   False

SCORING

To tally your score, give yourself 1 point for each response that matches yours. The higher your score, the more you tend to present yourself (on tests at least) as socially desirable.

1. *False* **2.** *True* **3.** *False* **4.** *False* **5.** *False* **6.** *True* **7.** *True* **8.** *True* **9.** *True* **10.** *True*

A score of 1–4 points: Low drive for social desirability

You lean toward being a non-conforming, social rebel. You try to appear different and independent of others and may indulge in too much self-flattery. It probably wouldn't bother you to be left out of a group.

A score of 5–8 points: Average drive for social desirability

You present yourself to others realistically. You are secure enough to show your faults as well as display your virtues.

A score of 9–10 points: High drive for social desirability

You probably seek the approval of others more than you should. You are quite shy about expressing yourself. Scorers in this range sometimes struggle with feelings of inferiority.

In this quiz neither an extremely low nor extremely high score is especially desirable. Either may indicate that you need more self-acceptance and greater insight in how you come across to others. In addition, you may want to consider the role of your own "private pride" in determining your score. You may find it difficult to be completely honest in your responses due to a desire to create a positive image of yourself in your own mind. Again, learning to accept yourself may help you to see yourself more clearly, and ultimately be more comfortable in your own skin.

EXPLANATION

This quiz measures social desirability, the human tendency to present ourselves in the way that best serves our goals. The introduction to this quiz is non-specific for a reason—had you been clued in to its purpose, it's likely your responses would have been biased.

Self-report tests like personality quizzes are subject to some scrutiny because there's always the chance that a person's answers might be colored by faulty memory, distorted recall, or just plain fudging. Occasionally people misrepresent themselves by "faking good," slanting their answers in order to make a positive impression. This might happen, for example, when people apply for a job. People "fake bad" when they present a negative image of themselves, just as an accident victim would when claiming compensation. Slanting answers in the direction of social desirability distorts a test's validity, and has been a concern for some time—the study of such "response bias" was begun more than forty years ago by Professor Lee J. Cronbach at the University of Illinois.

The situations provided in this assessment are similar to those found on tests that measure socially approved behavior. Responses of "False" to items 1 through 5 and "True" to 6 through 8 are probably not likely to be given in other, non-test environments. Whether a person gives "socially proper" answers or not does not reflect on his emotional stability or character, it simply reveals how he would like others to view him.

Are You a People Person or a Wallflower?

What makes people get up on stage when the call goes out for volunteers from the audience? Chances are they're extraverts—those who enjoy doing things with and for others.

As far back as 1921, Carl Jung, the Swiss psychoanalyst, first coined the terms introversion and extraversion. The notion that all of mankind could be divided into these two types has been around for several centuries, but Jung did the most extensive study and writing on the subject. He maintained that we are born with two "innate attitudes," one which focuses inwardly on ourselves and the other, outwardly toward others.

Jung felt that both of these tendencies exist in everyone. But one attitude gets the upper hand while the other lies submerged deep in the unconscious, exerting a counterforce that may show up in dreams and fantasies. So, according to Jung every extravert on the outside is an introvert on the inside, and vice versa.

While extraverts need heavy doses of social stimulation and are less interested in their inner experiences, such as feelings, imagination, and ideas, introverts are just the opposite.

One orientation is not healthier than the other, although different cultures may encourage one or the other. Introverts are among the world's best researchers, scientists, and writers, while extraverts excel as business managers, teachers, and salespeople.

TEST

If you wonder where you fall on the Introvert-Extravert scale, the following quiz might provide some clues.

1. I am more of a listener than a talker.

a. Very true *b. Largely true* *c. Slightly true*
d. Not True

2. Compared with others, I am difficult to get to know.

a. Very true *b. Largely true* *c. Slightly true*
d. Not True

3. I find it difficult or unpleasant to make small talk.

a. Very true *b. Largely true* *c. Slightly true*
d. Not True

4. I am a worrier.

a. Very true *b. Largely true* *c. Slightly true*
d. Not True

5. I would not want to be in charge of a large group.

a. Very true *b. Largely true* *c. Slightly true*
d. Not True

6. I would feel very self-conscious if someone pointed out a large stain on my clothes in front of other people.

a. Very true *b. Largely true* *c. Slightly true*
d. Not True

7. I have a tendency to daydream.
a. Very true   *b.* Largely true   *c.* Slightly true
d. Not True

8. It makes me feel uneasy when strangers watch me doing something.
a. Very true   *b.* Largely true   *c.* Slightly true
d. Not Irue

9. It takes me a long time to get over an embarrassment.
a. Very true   *b.* Largely true   *c.* Slightly true
d. Not True

10. I would feel embarrassed if I stumbled in public.
a. Very true   *b.* Largely true   *c.* Slightly true
d. Not True

SCORING

To tally your score, give yourself 1 point for each "a" response, 2 points for each "b" response, 3 points for each "c," and 4 points for each "d."

A score of 29–40 points: You are highly extraverted. You enjoy being around and interacting with people. However you may want to guard against acting too spontaneously in certain settings in which your gregarious side might best be kept under control.

A score of 21–28 points: You fall somewhere between both Introvert-Extravert extremes, as do most people. You like being part of the social set but you also enjoy time alone.

A score of 10–20 points: You tend to be on the introvertive side. You can cope with people when necessary but for the most part prefer to be alone. You're not highly dependent on others to uplift your mood, but instead tend to rely on your inner mental life for inspiration.

EXPLANATION

Western society tends to foster extravertive behavior. We approve of children who are outgoing and socially assertive and disapprove of the absence of these traits. In some non-occidental societies, however, introversion is a more acceptable personality style.

Professor Hans Eysenck, in his work at Maudsley Hospital in London, concluded that the introvert-extravert conflict is better explained in biological, rather than cultural terms. He believes introverts have a more sensitive nervous system than extraverts, causing them to withdraw in order to prevent their brains from being overwhelmed. Introverts tend to follow their own mind set and are not overly swayed by the opinions of others. Extraverts, on the other hand, physically require lots of stimulation, and actively seek out others whose opinions and ideas are influential.

Despite someone's natural propensity toward one extreme or the other, they can alternate between the two attitudes, depending upon the situation. For example, at a party someone who is generally introvertive may be more outgoing, talkative, and responsive if he or she knows the other guests. But if he or she knows no one except the hostess—who is busy taking coats and freshening drinks—the gregarious side of his or her personality may not surface as readily.

While each of these types possesses positive characteristics, extremes of either type can present problems in certain settings. The strong extravert needs contact and feedback from others, and grows restless when working or studying quietly alone. He yearns to be near others. A strong introvert seeks solitude and feels nervous when dealing with others even in the most casual way. As always, moderation is the key.

Do You Fight or Flee: How Confrontational Are You?

In the Stone Age, disagreements were settled with clubs. As our language capacity increased, we soon learned that disputes could be talked out, and this realization gave birth to the argument. The ability to formulate and conduct an argument is inherent in all of us, but it seems that some of us choose to flex this muscle more than others.

It's a familiar scene—you're confronted by a very aggressive person who argues seemingly without much provocation. He's the hot-headed, competitive type with well-honed scuffling skills, who provokes controversy simply for the sake of venting frustration. After you're ensnared in a row with him, you may wonder just how the scoundrel manipulated you into it.

But suppose it was only partially the scoundrel's doing? What if there was some degree of escalation on your part that got you sucked into the fracas? The question is, how susceptible are you to a quarrel? If you faced a scenario that signaled an upcoming argument, would you be prone to join the fray, or would you deftly avoid it?

TEST

This quiz measures susceptibility to confrontations. It is based on research done at Kent State University in Ohio by psychiatrists D. A. Infante and A. S. Rancer. Respond "True" or "False" to the items below to determine how eager you are to fight it out.

1. Arguing calmly over controversial issues sharpens one's logic.

True   False

2. When I argue I am usually concerned about whether my opponent will think I'm too dogmatic.

True   False

3. I feel a sense of energy and enthusiasm when I confront someone.

True   False

4. It upsets me to argue.

True   False

5. I enjoy using a good argument to put strongly self-assured people in their place.

True   False

6. I generally lose more quarrels than I win.

True   False

7. I find people who always agree with others to be somewhat dull.

True   False

8. I get nervous around argumentative people.

True   False

9. I don't have much respect for a person who won't fight for what he believes in.

True   False

10. When others are in a ruckus, I often play the role of pacifier.

True   False

11. I feel compelled to speak up for a point that I feel is valid.

True   False

12. I prefer being with people who don't disagree with me.

True   False

SCORING

To tally your score, give yourself 1 point for each response that matches yours.

1. *True* **2.** *False* **3.** *True* **4.** *False* **5.** *True* **6.** *False* **7.** *True* **8.** *False* **9.** *True* **10.** *False* **11.** *True* **12.** *False*

A score of 0–4: You are a peace-loving creature who likes harmony. Other people's strong emotions often upset you. You may be suppressing your true feelings too much, however, and might be better off expressing some of them occasionally.

A score of 5–7: You are about average in your susceptibility to arguments. You don't mind conflicts once in a while, even when they reach the point of anger, but for the most part you know when to back off and suffer fools gladly.

A score of 8–12: You are highly argumentative, a veritable tiger who won't let a strident statement go unchecked. Your biggest challenge may seem to be in dealing with someone as combative as you, but conflict with a less aggressive foe presents another set of trials, as you may leave egos irrevocably bruised. Learning to listen and let go instead of lunge and leap might help you avoid meaningless scuffles and, more importantly, marred relationships.

EXPLANATION

Research shows that there are two types of arguers, those who approach a battle ("hawks") and those who avoid it ("doves"). Hawks generally answer "True" to the odd-numbered items in this test, while doves typically answer "True" to the even-numbered items.

Do You Express Anger Constructively?

In many cultures, anger and aggression are not considered positive forces in human affairs. But no matter what an individual's culture, he must learn to channel his anger constructively. Unfortunately, few of us are taught how to do this.

There are times when one must communicate, if not act upon, one's angry feelings. The trouble is that many of us confuse anger (a feeling state) with aggression (an act of violence). And this inhibits us from asserting our opinions.

TEST

Do you confuse the expression of anger with aggression? Do you know how to show anger in a constructive manner? The following quiz may provide an answer.

1. I never or very rarely become angry.
a. Agree *b. Agree somewhat* *c. Disagree*

2. I avoid expressing anger, because most people would misinterpret it as hatred.
a. Agree *b. Agree somewhat* *c. Disagree*

3. To be honest, I would rather bury my resentment toward a friend than risk losing his or her acceptance.
a. Agree *b. Agree somewhat* *c. Disagree*

4. No one has ever won an argument by blowing up.
a. Agree *b. Agree somewhat* *c. Disagree*

5. It's better to work out my anger on my own than to disclose it to others.
a. Agree *b. Agree somewhat* *c. Disagree*

6. Anger is not a mature or noble way to react to a frustrating situation.
a. Agree *b. Agree somewhat* *c. Disagree*

7. It's probably not a good idea to discipline someone while you are angry with him or her.
a. Agree *b. Agree somewhat* *c. Disagree*

8. The expression of anger only begets more anger and adds to the problem.
a. Agree *b. Agree somewhat* *c. Disagree*

9. When angry, I usually hide it because I fear making a fool of myself.
a. Agree *b. Agree somewhat* *c. Disagree*

10. When angry with someone close to you, you should try to communicate it in some way, even if it is painful.
a. Agree *b. Agree somewhat* *c. Disagree*

SCORING

To tally your score, give yourself 1 point for each "a" response, 2 points for each "b" response, and 3 points for each "c."

A score of 24–30 points: You accept your angry feelings and recognize how they should be expressed to build better interpersonal relationships.

A score of 17–23 points: You have an average grasp of how and why one should express anger to "clear the air." But there is always room for improvement.

A score of 10–16 points: You don't handle your anger as well as you might in order to promote more solid relationships with others. Perhaps you feel guilty about even experiencing anger, especially when it's toward someone close to you. Keep in mind that it's better to express your anger in the moment than to fantasize later about retaliation.

EXPLANATION

There are two compelling reasons to express your anger constructively. First, it vents uncomfortable feelings of frustration, which, if allowed to fester, could cause one to retaliate unfairly; and second, it can be a method for motivating someone to modify his behavior.

But simply talking out a conflict with an adversary or even a "neutral" party may not reduce the ire—it may only rehearse it. When venting anger, it is important that it lead to mutual understanding, or else it will not be beneficial for both parties. When we confuse anger (an emotion) with aggression (an act of violence), it prevents us from showing our feelings.

Carol Tavris is the author of *Anger: The Misunderstood Emotion*. Tavris points out that airing a grievance can be a constructive experience for both persons only if it is done in a mature manner—the expression of anger doesn't have to bowl someone over. Rather, it can be modulated and expressed verbally as annoyance, displeasure, or chagrin. The purpose of discussing a transgression in the first place is to resolve any hurt feelings and insure that the problem doesn't recur. If we fail to communicate our anger, we won't shape our offender's behavior, and chances are that the act or comment we found obnoxious will be repeated.

Dr. George Bach, a California psychologist and marriage counselor, has worked with couples who show their anger destructively, through such non-physical assaults as passive aggression, sneak attacks, and verbal back-stabbing. He has concluded that couples who never learned to express anger constructively and therefore fight unfairly usually have poor relationships. Bach and many other experts believe that negative emotions like anger can be channeled in a positive manner. They urge people to exercise "creative aggression" whereby annoyances are expressed without demeaning the opponent or diminishing his or her self-esteem. This method allows both partners to be honest about their feelings without damaging their relationship. If "creative aggression" doesn't sound like your thing, and you prefer to turn the other cheek, just be sure that your opponent understands your position.

How Time-Conscious Are You?

Time sense differs around the world. The culture we live in shapes our attitudes about time, and gradually we set our inner clocks to conform to its tempo. Many tropical nations have a slower daily rhythm—while nations in northern climates tend to move much faster.

In his work at the California State University at Fresno, psychology professor Robert Levine surveyed a cross-section of nations (Japan, England, Italy, Indonesia, Taiwan, and the United States). He found that by many measures, Japan has the fastest pace of life, while Indonesia assumes the most relaxed attitude about timed activities.

TEST

In Western society we value promptness and are very focused on time. Those people who handle time efficiently tend to be in great demand and are generally successful in life. What pace do you set for yourself? The following quiz, similar to those used in the Stanford University Time Perspective Inventory, should help to gauge your sense of time urgency.

1. It bothers me when I am late for an appointment.
a. Rarely or very little   *b. Sometimes or moderately*
c. Often or very much

2. I am disoriented when I forget to wear my watch.
a. Rarely or very little   *b. Sometimes or moderately*
c. Often or very much

3. It is hard for me to let time go by and do absolutely nothing.
a. Rarely or very little   *b. Sometimes or moderately*
c. Often or very much

4. It irritates me to be kept waiting.
a. Rarely or very little   *b. Sometimes or moderately*
c. Often or very much

5. It is upsetting for me to put off finishing a task.
a. Rarely or very little   *b. Sometimes or moderately*
c. Often or very much

6. I make lists of things to do.
a. Rarely or very little   *b. Sometimes or moderately*
c. Often or very much

7. I am on time for appointments and meet deadlines and obligations that involve others.
a. Rarely or very little   *b. Sometimes or moderately*
c. Often or very much

8. I enjoy doing many things within a short period of time.
a. Rarely or very little   *b. Sometimes or moderately*
c. Often or very much

9. When I have a few hours on my hands I think of how to best use the time.
a. Rarely or very little   *b. Sometimes or moderately*
c. Often or very much

10. If I expect a long wait, I bring work or something to read.
a. Rarely or very little   *b. Sometimes or moderately*
c. Often or very much

11. I like to allocate blocks of time to specific projects.

a. *Rarely or very little* **b.** *Sometimes or moderately*
c. *Often or very much*

12. I carry a pad on which to jot down to-do lists.

a. *Rarely or very little* **b.** *Sometimes or moderately*
c. *Often or very much*

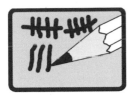

SCORING

To tally your score, give yourself 1 point for each "a" response, 2 points for each "b" response, and 3 points for each "c." Keep in mind that neither extreme of time consciousness is particularly beneficial when it comes to respecting your scheduling constraints. If you are too easygoing, you may miss the chance to accomplish worthwhile goals. If you are too driven to "honor" time, then you've made a potentially valuable personality trait into a liability.

A score of 12–19 points: You are time-carefree. You don't pay enough attention to the limits that time imposes on your life. You probably frustrate others by your lax attitude and low sense of time urgency. Strive to make and keep deadlines for completing tasks.

A score of 20–29 points: You have a sensible attitude about time and a realistic sense of urgency about getting things done when you should.

A score of 30–36 points: You are on your way to becoming a compulsive clock-watcher. Train yourself to put things into perspective and tackle important tasks first. Relax and get used to feeling comfortable with the idea that some things can be put off until tomorrow without dire consequences.

EXPLANATION

While culture affects our perception of time, being time-conscious is an individual matter. It doesn't depend on a timepiece on the wall. Our subjective clock can be habitually slower than objective time. So, in addition to our society's view of time, we are strict or lax about it depending on factors such as what we are doing at the moment, the people we are with, and our prevailing mood. Professor Levine and his associates found that people tend to live in different time frames. A few live in the past, some live in the present, and most live in the future. As teenagers, we live in the here and now, enjoying each passing hour as it arises. But as we grow to adulthood, we become more future-oriented, putting off immediate pleasures for the sake of future goals.

Those of us in Western society have a special preoccupation with what lies ahead. Our savings banks and insurance companies thrive on fostering a sense of an extended future. But any extreme time perspective could work against us. The mismanagement of time is usually a significant factor in what causes much of our stress. We give ourselves only a limited period in which to accomplish our goals and often miscalculate how much time we'll really need.

Alan Lakein, time consultant and the author of *How to Get Control of Your Time and Your Life,* advises that we prioritize the things we do. In order to minimize stress and maximize productivity, we should give top billing to the most crucial tasks, then work our way down the list to the least-important projects.

Are Thrills Your Thing?

The statement "truth is stranger than fiction" may be a cliché, but it tells it best. A few years ago a twenty-nine-year-old student from Long Beach, California, pushed his hang glider off a cliff and promptly slammed to earth six hundred feet below. He wasn't wearing a helmet. After several days spent near death in an intensive care unit, he was discharged from the hospital and soon returned to his favorite sport—hang gliding.

Why do people take chances? Humans, it seems, have an unexplained urge for stimulation. Call it thrill seeking, if you will—it exists in degrees in every person, from high-wire artists to children on skateboards. The appetite for thrills peaks in our teens, then gradually decreases as we grow older, but some of us never quite lose the desire to experience new and exciting kicks.

Dr. Marvin Zuckerman calls this phenomenon "sensation seeking." He believes it is a universal trait that probably has a biological basis. Through extensive research, Zuckerman has devised a number of questionnaires that identify those who actively seek to bombard their senses as a means of sparking up their lives. For these people, paths to the sensational could include such simple activities as ordering an exotic dish, speeding, or reading adventure stories instead of romance novels.

TEST

To test your sensation-seeking tendencies, try the following quiz. It is based on one of Dr. Zuckerman's tests.

1. I enjoy stories about medical breakthroughs.
a. Disagree   *b. Agree*   *c. Strongly agree*

2. When on a vacation trip, I prefer to camp out.
a. Disagree   *b. Agree*   *c. Strongly agree*

3. I would enjoy work that requires a lot of travel.
a. Disagree   *b. Agree*   *c. Strongly agree*

4. On a hot day, I like jumping into the ocean or a cold pool.
a. Disagree   *b. Agree*   *c. Strongly agree*

5. I enjoy spicy foods.
a. Disagree   *b. Agree*   *c. Strongly agree*

6. I would enjoy working to help people solve problems.
a. Disagree   *b. Agree*   *c. Strongly agree*

7. I prefer scary movies.
a. Disagree   *b. Agree*   *c. Strongly agree*

8. I enjoy being out on a cold day.
a. Disagree   *b. Agree*   *c. Strongly agree*

9. I get bored seeing the same familiar faces.
a. Disagree   *b. Agree*   *c. Strongly agree*

10. I like emotionally expressive people even if they're eccentric or somewhat unstable.
a. Disagree   *b. Agree*   *c. Strongly agree*

11. I would enjoy being hypnotized.

a. Disagree *b.* Agree *c.* Strongly agree

12. I would prefer working on a commission basis to being on salary.

a. Disagree *b.* Agree *c.* Strongly agree

SCORING

To tally your score, give yourself 1 point for each "a" response, 2 points for each "b" response, and 3 points for each "c."

A score of 30–36 points: You are a thrill seeker.

A score of 20–29 points: You have about average needs for adventure and new sensations.

A score of 12–19 points: You are somewhat conservative in your tastes and less daring than most people.

EXPLANATION

Most sensation seekers answer the items as true of themselves. Compared to the average, they tend to be more adaptable to fast-moving situations and show strong preferences for entering the helping professions such as medicine, social service, and teaching.

After some forty years of work, Dr. Zuckerman concluded that very high scorers differ from low scorers in four basic ways:

1. Thrill and adventure seeking: They look for new thrills by engaging in risky and adventurous activities such as sky diving, riding roller coasters, and motorcycling.

2. Experience seeking: They continually seek excitement by adopting a non-conventional style, i.e., by making unusual (eccentric) friends, traveling frequently, or taking drugs.

3. Disinhibition: They tend to be socially uninhibited and are drawn to social drinking, gambling, and sexual experimentation.

4. Boredom susceptibility: They have low tolerance for experiences that are constant or repetitious, such as routine work or association with predictable, "boring" people.

In the journal *Psychology Today*, Professor Frank Farley reported experiments that demonstrate thrill seekers' need to maintain a high level of arousal in their nervous system. Sometimes called "adrenaline junkies," these people choose to be hyped up rather than calmed down. Males tend to dominate this category. Because men often equate risk-taking with courage, they generally score higher than women on assessments of thrill-seeking levels. This can be attributed in part to social attitudes: Boys are encouraged to take chances and engage in risky behavior more often than girls. When it comes to thrill seeking, this gender split tends to bear out.

Could You Become Assaultive?

When laboratory animals receive electrical shocks they tend to vent their anger by pouncing on those nearby. The effects of frustration on human behavior are not much different. Our frustration often spells trouble for others, especially those closest to us.

Handling hostile impulses is a never-ending, lifelong challenge. Unfortunately, some of us never quite adopt a satisfactory way of managing our hostility. The evidence shows that we learn to be aggressive in stages. As a child one may strike a playmate or parent during a tantrum. But if this type of behavior persists later in life, it can spill over into everyday situations in undesirable proportions. It is through a lifetime of learning that violence is adopted as a solution to social conflicts.

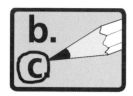

TEST

The following quiz is based on the findings of Dr. Richard Parlour and others who have written about aggressive behavior. It may help to gauge your susceptibility to being assaultive.

1. I fall into moods of irritability for no apparent reason.
a. Rarely   *b. Sometimes*   *c. Often*

2. I don't work hard enough to improve myself.
a. Rarely   *b. Sometimes*   *c. Often*

3. If someone yells at me, I yell right back.
a. Rarely   *b. Sometimes*   *c. Often*

4. I drink frequently and often get drunk.
a. Rarely   *b. Sometimes*   *c. Often*

5. I do things on impulse.
a. Rarely   *b. Sometimes*   *c. Often*

6. When others cross me, I don't forgive and forget easily.
a. Rarely   *b. Sometimes*   *c. Often*

7. When I'm angry, I slam or break things.
a. Rarely   *b. Sometimes*   *c. Often*

8. I engage in physical activity or use some other outlet to "let off steam."
a. Rarely   *b. Sometimes*   *c. Often*

9. If someone annoys me, I'm quick to tell them off.
a. Rarely   *b. Sometimes*   *c. Often*

10. After an outburst I regret having lost my temper.
a. Rarely   *b. Sometimes*   *c. Often*

SCORING

To tally your score, give yourself 1 point for each "a" response, 2 points for each "b" response, and 3 points for each "c."

A score of 10–14 points: You tend to express your anger peacefully, but may suppress it on occasion.

A score of 15–21 points: You have an average amount of control when it comes to inhibiting your angry feelings.

A score of 22–30 points: You have a short fuse when under stress and may want to exercise more self-control. It might help to review the items that you responded "Often" to and try to work on changing those behaviors.

EXPLANATION

In his work, Dr. Parlour found that destructive actions are common in our society. He identified early predictors of aggressive outbreaks, some of which are in our quiz. He concluded that each of us has a breaking point and that if enough stress is placed on us, we are likely to vent our anger in an aggressive way. But Parlour is quick to note that too often those who act out attribute their behavior to some sort of "last straw," when actually we all have much more self-restraint than we realize.

Can psychologists predict an outbreak of anger in a family? Dr. J. Monahan, author of *The Clinical Prediction of Criminal Behavior,* says that it is not possible to predict violence with much accuracy. However, he notes, there are some characteristics that help predict whether a husband might strike his wife. They include whether the husband himself had a history of family violence, whether his peers were violent, and whether he has had a history of steady unemployment. Monahan advises that people with the tendency to act out steer clear of situations that might trigger impulsive behavior.

Our quiz is based on a list of traits that correlate with poor self-control. Some experts believe that giving in too easily to "alien" impulses is behavior learned through role models, such as parents, siblings, or peers, in our formative years. But it must be said that most domestic upsets do not involve violence.

It is important to note that if you have the potential to anger quickly, it is always intensified by alcohol. At Yale University, professor A. B. Hollingshead did a survey of five hundred divorce cases and found that more than 26 percent of the complaints filed were based on excessive drinking by a spouse, usually the husband.

Prejudice: Does It Have You in Its Grip?

W e've seen it time and again: The front page tells a sordid tale of a victim of discrimination, or worse, a hate crime. It seems that no matter how far we progress as a society we are still plagued by prejudice. In studies at Harvard University, psychologists Hadley Cantril and Gordon Allport spent considerable time researching this most terrible form of inhumanity. The results of their seminal work, which have been verified many times, disclose a number of characteristics of the bigoted personality.

According to their findings, we're most susceptible to scapegoating others for our woes when we're down and out, whether that means being angry, frustrated, unfulfilled, or heavily in debt. What's more, we're likely to be unaware of these actions and the pain they cause.

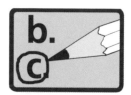

TEST

Do you harbor prejudiced notions about others without realizing it? The following quiz should help you see more clearly.

1. After all the facts have been collected and sorted out, there is really only one right answer to any question.
True   False

2. I would rank myself as strongly traditional and conservative in my attitudes.
True   False

3. I am in direct competition socially, educationally, and/or occupationally with people of other backgrounds.
True   False

4. I have always had difficulty achieving financial success.
True   False

5. I have had less formal education than most people.
True   False

6. I often wish for great psychological power and strength.
True   False

7. I lean towards severe punishment and a generally hard line of discipline for criminal offenders.
True   False

8. I tend to be more suspicious than my friends of other people's motives.
True   False

9. I know very little about people from other ethnic backgrounds.
True   False

10. Compared with most parents, mine were strict and demanding.
True   False

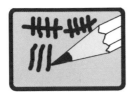

SCORING

To tally your score, give yourself 1 point for each "True" answer.

A score of 1–3 points: You are mature, tolerant, and relatively free of prejudice. You have a live-and-let-live attitude toward others.

A score of 4–7 points: You have an average number of biased attitudes. Remember, there is always some room for improvement.

A score of 8–10 points: Move over Archie Bunker. You tend to come to prejudicial conclusions about others. One way to combat this is to learn more about those you prejudge. You may be surprised to discover that they struggle with many of the same life problems that you do.

EXPLANATION

People who generally respond "True" to the items on this quiz tend to have more prejudicial viewpoints. Here's an item-by-item analysis:

1. *True.* People who are partial often take a hard stand on either side of a question. They often have little tolerance for ambiguity. They are frustrated by uncertainty and like to see issues as clear cut without shades of gray in between.

2. *True.* Prejudiced persons are more likely than not to be status-quo thinkers with traditional values. They usually conform to conservative customs and accept innovation with reluctance.

3. *True.* Groups who are in competition with each other tend to have biased views about each other as well. Competitors are often seen as enemies who threaten to thwart a group's progress.

4. *True.* The temptation to scapegoat someone for one's frustration is strongest when facing adversity. Historical records support this, showing an increase in outbreaks of racial discrimination during hard times.

5. *True.* In general, those who have had little schooling tend to be more discriminatory in their attitudes than those who are more educated.

6. *True.* Bigotry is often found in those with a "will to power," who enjoy mastery over others. These people strongly reject those who are outside their group. Extreme examples of this "ethnomania" are Julius Caesar, Adolf Hitler, and Slobodan Milosevic.

7. *True.* Harsh disciplinarians are more likely to hold biased views of others. They expect punishment for their misdeeds and, at the same time, are not apt to be lenient with those who break the law.

8. *True.* Those who carry prejudiced notions tend to be doubtful of other people's integrity and honesty. They have a basic distrust of strangers and see the world as an unsafe place.

9. *True.* The less we know and understand about the targets of our prejudice, the more likely we are to harbor preconceived ideas about them.

10. *True.* High scorers on prejudice questionnaires tend to come from rigid families with parents who are stern disciplinarians and sticklers for rules and regulations.

Author Ben Hecht once wrote that prejudice is a raft onto which the shipwrecked mind clambers and paddles to safety. Prejudice is a general trait much like assertiveness, for example, and if we suffer from it, it colors much of our thinking. Thus, a person who is biased against one group tends to be biased against other groups as well.

If others pose a threat, real or imagined, to our security, it is human nature to scapegoat them. But as most of us understand, just because something may be natural doesn't mean it's right. One of Katherine Hepburn's lines in the movie *The African Queen* gives us our lead. When Humphrey Bogart tries to excuse his vices as "only part of [his] human nature," Ms. Hepburn replies crisply, "My dear sir, human nature is precisely what we are put on earth to overcome."

Can You Keep Yourself in Check?

A hard-bitten oil tycoon was once asked if he had stomach ulcers. His reply, " I don't get ulcers, I give them." Living intensely is a way of life for some people. More than 80 million prescriptions for tranquilizers are written annually to help us keep our emotions in check, but still some of us don't succeed. Our blow-ups often cause detrimental results for ourselves and for others.

Researchers have devised lengthy questionnaires designed to identify individuals who don't handle stress well. The following quiz is based on studies by Leonard Derogatis at Johns Hopkins University, which assess your style of handling difficult situations.

TEST

To determine if you are likely to drop a bomb when irritated, take the following test.

1. You grow quite impatient when you must wait in line.
a. Rarely *b. Sometimes* *c. Often*

2. You work very hard, play very hard, and try to be the best at what you do.
a. Rarely *b. Sometimes* *c. Often*

3. You easily become annoyed when held up by someone in traffic.
a. Rarely *b. Sometimes* *c. Often*

4. You are more of a go-getter than most of your friends.
a. Rarely *b. Sometimes* *c. Often*

5. You slam and break things when angry.
a. Rarely *b. Sometimes* *c. Often*

6. It irritates you when people don't take their job seriously.
a. Rarely *b. Sometimes* *c. Often*

7. You snap at strangers when you become annoyed, for example while driving, shopping or working.
a. *Rarely*   *b.* *Sometimes*   *c.* *Often*

8. You become angered when you fail at things you attempt to do.
a. *Rarely*   *b.* *Sometimes*   *c.* *Often*

9. When angry, you speed up and do things like driving, eating, and walking faster.
a. *Rarely*   *b.* *Sometimes*   *c.* *Often*

10. You don't easily forgive and forget someone who has offended you.
a. *Rarely*   *b.* *Sometimes*   *c.* *Often*

SCORING

To tally your score, give yourself 1 point for each "a" response, 2 points for each "b" response, and 3 points for each "c." The higher you score, the more you tend to be an intensive adaptor to daily life.

A score of 0–15 points: You are low-key and easy-going.

A score of 16–23 points: You are in the average range of emotional response to life's ups and downs.

A score of 24–30 points: You're living in a pressure cooker. It's time to ease up, relax, and gain a better perspective on your life.

EXPLANATION

The items included in the quiz generally depict over-reactions to fairly typical situations. They display an intensity that is usually not needed to cope with the matters at hand.

A healthy personality engages in a kind of psychic economy of its own. It responds to life with the effort and energy reasonably appropriate to deal with events—not much more and not much less. Here are just a few examples at the other extreme: a homemaker who jumps up and rushes to answer the doorbell every time it rings, a teenager who gulps his food, a manager who slams her desk or repeatedly jabs the elevator button. These are all over-extended behaviors. Psychologists look for this "too muchness" quality and typically judge it as neurotic.

It's fair to say that occasionally everyone acts intensively, but just because someone exhibits this behavior doesn't necessarily mean that he or she is maladjusted. However, some high-tension types actually unwittingly strive to maintain a constant level of stress. These so-called "adrenaline junkies" spew more of the stuff than most of us. To them, life just isn't exciting unless it is lived in a state of urgency.

Work at Harvard University shows that high-tension types drive hard to gain mastery over their lives. They are argumentative, competitive, and over-sensitive to slights by others (as touched upon in quiz items 3, 6, and 10). They make up for shortcomings by overcompensating (see items 2, 4, and 8) and they tend to scapegoat others as well (items 1, 5, 7, and 9).

Do You Have What It Takes to Be Funny?

There is a big difference between having a sense of humor and being able to make people laugh. A hearty sense of humor requires a readiness to spot and respond to comedy when it is offered to you. This doesn't necessarily make you a good joke teller, though. The ability to deliver a funny tale requires other, more sophisticated, traits. These include flexibility, social maturity, intelligence, high empathy, and, of course, a good sense of humor.

TEST

Take the following quiz to determine whether you have the capacity to be a comedic cut-up.

1. I consider myself more of an extravert than an introvert.

True   False

2. I sometimes make faces at myself in the mirror.

True   False

3. In a slapstick movie sequence, I prefer slow-motion pictures to those in fast motion.

True   False

4. I become upset when the joke is on me.

True   False

5. Most photos of me aren't really true to life.

True   False

6. I tend to remember many jokes.

True   False

7. At the zoo, I prefer watching lions and tigers rather than monkeys and apes.

True   False

8. I'm usually socially uninhibited.

True   False

9. I would enjoy entertaining others by singing, dancing, or telling an anecdote about myself.

True   False

10. Make a small doodle right now. See the "Explanation" section of this quiz (page 33) to find out what it says about you.

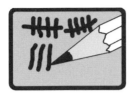

SCORING

To tally your score, give yourself 1 point for each response to items 1 through 9 that matches yours, and 1 point if your doodle for item 10 contains mostly curved lines.

1. *True* **2.** *True* **3.** *False* **4.** *False* **5.** *False* **6.** *True* **7.** *False* **8.** *True* **9.** *True*

A score of 8–10 points: You are comfortable with your sense of humor and are quite a comedian.

A score of 4–7 points: You have an average ability to make others laugh.

A score of 0–3 points: You may take yourself too seriously to be a clown or a card. Perhaps you are self-conscious about being the center of attention. Try to let go a bit and enjoy yourself more.

Note: No matter what your score, keep in mind that your delivery of humor improves with practice. Remind yourself to look for the light side of things as you go through each day. Doing so will make you and others happier and will also help you handle stress better.

EXPLANATION

The correct answers in this quiz are based on the responses that were given most often by those with a high sense of humor. An item-by-item explanation of the quiz follows.

1. *True.* Humor is a socially shared experience and someone who is oriented toward others tends to have a high sense of humor. This is an essential trait for good joke tellers.

2. *True.* If you can be playful and see yourself as another person might see you, you have "detachment," the ability to be objective about yourself. This is an important quality in bringing humor to others—it indicates flexibility and the inclination to look at the light side of things.

3. *False.* Slow-motion pictures are usually used to emphasize aesthetic and scientific details while those in fast-motion are generally used to evoke laughter.

4. *False.* Accepting self-contradictions is highly correlated with sense of humor. It shows a healthy, non-critical attitude.

5. *False.* People who reject objective reflections of themselves are often inflexible, take themselves too seriously, and tend to have a limited sense of humor.

6. *True.* Those people who possess the talent to tell funny stories can usually recall many jokes as well. They are proactive types who initiate as well as respond to humor. But those who have both a good memory for jokes and a willingness to relate them make good comics.

7. *False.* There is a greater similarity between humans and apes than between humans and felines. Finding amusement in simian antics rather than those of lions or tigers indicates a willingness to laugh at yourself, which is often true of funny people.

8. *True.* An uninhibited willingness to be open is a trait that most joke tellers have in common.

9. *True.* The desire to entertain others suggests that you are comfortable being in the spotlight and receive social admiration well.

10. Curved or wavy lines are indicative of a more flexible personality than straight or angular lines. The latter suggests tenseness and rigid thinking, while curves show an open and playful nature.

The jokester enjoys others' enjoyment—an audience's laughter, applause, and praise boosts his ego and reinforces his acceptance by others.

But comedy doesn't just make the comedian feel good, it benefits the audience as well. There is some recent evidence that humor has a healing quality. More and more, humor is being used judiciously in psychotherapy to help ease the pain of trauma and put seemingly negative experiences in their proper perspective.

Do Your Parents' Hang-Ups Psych You Out?

How would you compare yourself with your parents on traits like sociability, assertiveness, and optimism? If you rate yourself as very similar to them, you might be tempted to conclude that your personality is inherited. But, aside from genes, your own experiences have also had much to do with shaping who you are.

It's a centuries-old question: Is nature or nurture more responsible for human development? This debate really kicked into high gear after Charles Darwin published *On the Origin of the Species* in 1859, in which he held that inheritance plays a significant role in determining a being's characteristics. Darwin theorized that advantageous physiological mutations naturally propagate themselves by enabling beings to survive and procreate, thereby passing along adaptations to subsequent generations.

Years later, in sharp contrast, Johns-Hopkins University behaviorist J. B. Watson argued that one's characteristics are imparted more than inherited. He remarked that given a dozen healthy infants (from various backgrounds), he'd guarantee he could turn them into doctors, lawyers, beggars, or thieves.

Our view of genetics is much more sophisticated now than it was then. Today, for example, we study identical twins who've been separated at birth to determine what personality traits they share. Comparative studies have also been conducted with orphans, adoptive families, and fraternal twins. Some of the findings are included in the following quiz.

TEST

How much do you think you've inherited from your parents? Take the following quiz to find out.

1. An insecure mother's thoughts and beliefs can influence the character of her unborn infant.

True   False

2. People are born with an urge to be aggressive.

True   False

3. We inherit our ability in art, music, and sports.

True   False

4. Psychoneurosis, or more seriously, insanity, is caused by genes.

True   False

5. An aversion to snakes, bats, bugs, etc., is instinctive (i.e., not learned).

True   False

6. If close relatives marry, their children will be in some way underdeveloped.

True   False

7. How excitable or emotional I am depends upon the disposition I inherited from my parents.

True   False

8. Competitiveness is instinctive in human nature.

True   False

9. Girls usually inherit more traits from their mothers than from their fathers.

True   False

10. We can inherit our parent's alcoholism.

True   False

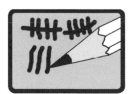

SCORING

To tally your score, give yourself 1 point for each "False" response.

A score of 1–5: You may think that many of your quirks and idiosyncrasies were genetic gifts, but they probably owe more to where you've been, what you've done, and who you've known than to your DNA.

A score of 6 points or more: You have a good grasp of what is or isn't inherited from your folks.

EXPLANATION

The evidence shows that our life experience determines much of who we are. An item-by-item explanation of the quiz follows.

1. *False.* An expectant mother's insecurity probably will not influence her baby. But the emotions she experiences, such as elation, depression, or fear, will temporarily affect her fetus's physiology through her nervous system and hormone levels.

2. *False.* We do not have an "aggression" gene. Rather, it is societies that engender aggression and even violence in their children, or teach them to avoid it.

3. *False.* We may inherit the physiology that gives us a predisposition to excel at art (like strong eye receptors for increased color perception) or music (such as sensitive auditory neurons for greater tone discrimination) but that is about all. The actual talent must then be trained and developed.

4. *False.* Some mental illnesses have a strong hereditary component (for example, certain neurological disorders and forms of epilepsy and psychosis), but the vast majority of mental disturbances are the result of life experiences.

5. *False.* Our specific fears are not inherited but are more likely adopted from those around us who displayed particular fear reactions to certain stimuli.

6. *False.* There is no strong evidence that underdevelopment results when parents are closely related.

7. *False.* This is true of animals but not of humans. Much of how we respond in the face of stress will depend upon how our role models (mostly our parents) reacted when confronted with stress.

8. *False.* Competitiveness is culturally acquired and not passed on through the genes.

9. *False.* A child will not always identify with the same sex parent. If a girl tends to act more like her mother than her father, chances are that she spent more time with her mother and modeled herself after her.

10. *False.* Alcoholism is not genetically caused. In families where drinking is frequent, a child may learn to use it as a remedy for frustration as others around him have done.

So, if you ever wonder whether your hang-ups have been handed down to you, think again. You're probably not the innocent victim of your genes. Chances are you yourself played the major role in the formation of your weaknesses. Incidentally, this goes for your strengths as well. One way to explain genetic influence is to say that our genes set the limits of our abilities and traits and our own experience does the rest.

CHAPTER 2

In the Mood for Love

*"I don't know what it's all about, but we seem to be in on the
ground floor of something or other."*

Are You the Jealous Type?

Love has many spin-offs. When Cupid's arrow strikes, it often brings with it a potentially troublesome emotion—jealousy. That green-eyed beast, which lies dormant in the darkest reaches of the loving heart, is portrayed in movies, poems, and novels as rearing its ugly head.

Jealousy appears in us at a tender age—around the middle of our second year—and resurfaces repeatedly throughout our lives. It's a pretty normal reaction to actual or imagined loss of affection from a valued one. It appears when we feel insecure about someone's esteem or love for us.

Here are some facts on the subject.

✔ Jealousy is more common among first-born children, who show it more intensely than those born later.

✔ It is more frequent in smaller families (those with two or three children) than in larger ones.

✔ It is more likely to occur among girls than boys, is stronger between sisters and occurs about equally among men and women.

✔ It is more prevalent in some cultures than others.

This last point may surprise you, but jealousy does exist to greater or lesser degrees in some societies. For example, it is rare in the Todas people of southern India, who discourage possessiveness. In contrast, the Apaches of North America have a traditionally jealous culture—historically, if a man had to leave his home for any reason, he would appoint a guard to watch his wife and children in his absence.

Everyone is subject to this "green" emotion, of course. It exists within our hearts, and we are all tempted by its lure. If the circumstances were compellingly stacked against you, how much of an "Othello" complex would you exhibit?

TEST

Each of the following situations involves a cohabitating couple. Try to imagine yourself and someone you love in each situation, and rate how upset, disturbed, or annoyed you might feel.

1. You're at a lively party, surrounded by attractive people, and you haven't seen your mate for over an hour.

a. *Not upset*   **b.** *A little upset*   **c.** *Moderately upset*
d. *Very upset*   **e.** *Extremely upset*

2. An unmarried old flame calls your mate and would like to meet him/her one evening for a drink and some conversation.

a. *Not upset*   **b.** *A little upset*   **c.** *Moderately upset*
d. *Very upset*   **e.** *Extremely upset*

3. Your mate has a hobby that you don't share. He/she has a full-time job, and in addition spends two weekday evenings and most of Saturday engaging in this hobby, while you stay at home or do other things.

a. *Not upset*   **b.** *A little upset*   **c.** *Moderately upset*
d. *Very upset*   **e.** *Extremely upset*

4. Your mate and a co-worker of the opposite sex are good friends, enjoying occasional lunches together and providing each other with emotional support on personal matters. Although your partner talks about this friend often, you do not know him/her well.

a. *Not upset*   **b.** *A little upset*   **c.** *Moderately upset*
d. *Very upset*   **e.** *Extremely upset*

5. You and your mate are very much in love, yet he/she has had two meetings with an ex. Your partner explains that he/she still cares about this person, finds him/her intellectually stimulating, and wants to see him/her occasionally.

a. *Not upset*   **b.** *A little upset*   **c.** *Moderately upset*
d. *Very upset*   **e.** *Extremely upset*

6. At a party, you discover your partner in an isolated spot kissing someone he/she met a few hours ago. Later your mate explains: "I had a bit too much to drink. It didn't mean anything." How would you feel?

a. *Not upset*   **b.** *A little upset*   **c.** *Moderately upset*
d. *Very upset*   **e.** *Extremely upset*

7. You've been trying to phone your partner for over an hour, but the line has been busy. Later your partner tells you he/she was talking to a mutual acquaintance whom you know to be flirtatious, and sometimes promiscuous. How would you feel?

a. *Not upset*   **b.** *A little upset*   **c.** *Moderately upset*
d. *Very upset*   **e.** *Extremely upset*

8. At a party your partner spends about an hour dancing with an attractive divorcée. You don't feel like dancing, and prefer to sit and chat with friends. How do you feel?

a. *Not upset*   **b.** *A little upset*   **c.** *Moderately upset*
d. *Very upset*   **e.** *Extremely upset*

SCORING

To tally your score, give yourself 1 point for each "a" response, 2 points for each "b" response, 3 points for each "c," 4 points for each "d," and 5 points for each "e."

A score of 0–19: It takes a lot to make you feel jealous. You're secure in the belief that your mate will be faithful to you. You should be careful, however, not to feel overly confident about the stability of human passions in tempting situations.

A score of 20–27: You have an average jealousy potential. If the tables were reversed in the above situations, you'd probably be true to your partner.

A score of 28 points or more: You tend to be the jealous type. Try to understand why. Do you fear being deserted? Are you unsure you can keep your mate interested in you?

EXPLANATION

There is a debate among behavioral scientists about the origins of jealousy: Is it inherited or do we develop it? Psychologists E. Aronson and A. Pines believe it is the latter. They developed an extensive 200-item sexual-jealousy questionnaire that was administered to several hundred subjects. Aronson and Pines found that jealous persons reported more overall dissatisfaction with their lives than others did. In addition, they tended to have a lower level of education, greater feelings of inferiority, and an unflattering self-image.

Are You Free to Fall in Love?

Like it or not, trust is a condition for survival in human society. Even in such simple acts as eating a candy or boarding a bus we have to trust that the candy hasn't been tampered with, or that the bus's brakes have been checked. The bottom line is that enjoying the benefits of societal living requires that we build a believing dependence upon one another. And, in our sometimes impersonal world, being trusted may well represent a greater compliment than being loved.

Obviously, your willingness to trust others depends upon the setting. You might trust a stranger at a professional function more readily than you would at a bar. Placing your faith in someone depends upon judgment as well. You might rely on a friend to feed your pet in your absence but would not trust the same friend to keep a secret. Yet trusting isn't completely reliant on setting or judgment.

At Tufts University in Medford, Massachusetts, psychologists C. Johnson-George and W. Swap identified a general personality trait they call "interpersonal trust"—it applies to one's ability to fall in love. Their extensive investigations found that women are more willing to trust others than men (though this need not suggest that people should be categorized as trusting or untrusting by gender alone). They also concluded that if you approach a relationship with a high level of distrust, it will probably be harder for you to trust unconditionally and fall in love. Of course, the amount you confide in and depend on other people can vary over time—a reluctance to trust at one point in your life may be in response to a variety of factors and does not mean you'll be that way forever.

TEST

If you are wondering whether you have the capacity to fall in love, the quiz below may provide some insight. It's based on the research at Tufts. Respond "True" or "False" to each item below to determine your "love-trust index."

1. I am reluctant to lend money to others because of the hassle often involved in getting it back.

True   False

2. Most people who compliment others are only flattering them for their own gains and don't really mean what they say.

True   False

3. The majority of people would intentionally misrepresent their point of view if it benefited them.

True   False

4. Most people who borrow something and return it slightly damaged probably wouldn't mention it to their lender.

True   False

5. Most people today are too dependent on others.

True   False

6. In general, I can take people or leave them.

True   False

7. If a company told its employees that profits were too low to grant pay raises, I would tend to doubt the firm's honesty.

True   False

8. Most politicians have taken bribes in some form or another.

True   False

9. Most successful people get ahead more as a result of *whom* they know than *what* they know.

True   False

10. People today tend to have lower moral standards than people a generation ago.

True   False

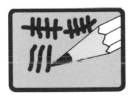

SCORING

To tally your score, give yourself 1 point for each "False" response.

A score of 8–10: You are a trusting person who accepts others as you see them. You fall in love easily. You may have a tendency to be so accepting of others that you are gullible or naïve.

A score of 5–7: You have a balance between trust and caution. You're open to new relationships but can maintain a fair amount of objectivity when it comes to trusting others and falling in love.

A score of 0–4: You are more guarded and suspicious than most people. You probably analyze others' motives too much. Your desire to protect yourself at all costs may prevent you from having meaningful relationships with honest people who deserve your trust.

EXPLANATION

Interpersonal trust involves risk. When beginning a friendship or romantic relationship, people often wonder if the possible gain will outweigh the chance of betrayal or rejection. After much research, Dr. Carl Rogers—

founder of the humanist movement in psychology and the former director of the Center for the Study of the Human Person in La Jolla, California—concluded that a measure of trust is fundamental to being a balanced individual. Realistic trust and a willingness to accept others usually indicate self-acceptance, and are signs of a well-adjusted personality.

Will You Reveal Who You Really Are?

Psychoanalyst Erik H. Erikson has described learning to trust as the earliest human conflict—one that even babies must grapple with. As we near adulthood, this conflict comes to envelop questions of physical intimacy, and later, falling in love. For some of us, however, the dilemma persists, and shapes whether we become someone who is open to others or someone who is emotionally closed.

In our fast-paced society, self-disclosure isn't always easy. But despite the fact that it might be an unsettling experience, it's a risk we must take in order to have meaningful interpersonal relationships.

TEST

Will you permit those closest to you to know who you truly are? Or will you remain an enigma, and perhaps appear to be someone you're not? Which of the following emotions and opinions would you reveal?

1. A consistent personality characteristic that you perceive as a weakness, such as a tendency to be jealous, obsessive, or obstinate.

a. I would not disclose this—I'm afraid of how someone might react.

b. I would hint at this, but not reveal it fully.

c. I would confide about this to a large degree.

d. I would tell all—what's the use in hiding how I feel?

2. Your pet peeves and prejudices about certain "types" of people (i.e., people of different religious, racial, or social backgrounds).

a. I would not disclose this—I'm afraid of how someone might react.

b. I would talk about this a little, but only if I felt that some of my opinions might be shared.

c. I would talk about this to a large extent.

d. I would discuss this openly. I'm not ashamed of my opinions.

3. Intimate details about your love life, including anecdotes about sex and your partner.

a. I would not disclose this—I'm afraid of how someone might react.

b. I would hint at this, but not reveal it fully.

c. I would confide about this to a large degree.

d. I would tell all.

4. Things you may have done that you're ashamed of or feel guilty about, such as cheating, lying, or committing a petty crime, such as shoplifting.

a. I would not disclose this—I'm afraid of how someone might react.

b. *I would hint at this, but not reveal it fully.*

c. *I would confide about this to a large degree.*

d. *I would tell all—I'm not going to hide my past.*

5. What really makes your blood boil—especially things that might seem inconsequential, such as long lines, telemarketers, or rude waiters.

a. *I would not disclose this—I'm afraid of how someone might react.*

b. *I would hint at this, but not reveal it fully.*

c. *I would confide about this to a large degree.*

d. *I would tell all—what's the use in hiding how I feel?*

6. How you feel about your appearance and sex appeal.

a. *I would not disclose this—I'd be too embarrassed.*

b. *I would hint at this, but not reveal it fully.*

c. *I would confide about this to a large degree.*

d. *I would tell all.*

7. The things you worry about most, even illogical fears.

a. *I would not disclose this—I'm afraid of how someone might react.*

b. *I would hint at this, but not reveal it fully.*

c. *I would confide about this to a large degree.*

d. *I would tell all.*

8. Your achievements, talents, and the compliments that you've received.

a. *I would not disclose this—I'm afraid of how someone might react.*

b. *I would hint at this, but not reveal it fully.*

c. *I would confide about this to a large degree.*

d. *I would tell all.*

9. Impulses you fear will get out of control if you "let go," such as drinking, gambling, sex, or anger.

a. *I would not disclose this—I'm afraid of what someone might think of me.*

b. *I would hint at this, but not reveal it fully.*

c. *I would confide about this to a large degree.*

d. *I would tell all.*

10. What you regard as a personal handicap, such as poor conversational skills, or lack of firmness.

a. *I would not disclose this—I'm afraid of how someone might react.*

b. *I would hint at this, but not reveal it fully.*

c. *I would confide about this to a large degree.*

d. *I would tell all.*

SCORING

To tally your score, give yourself 1 point for each "a" response, 2 points for each "b" response, 3 points for each "c," and 4 points for each "d."

A score of 10–17: You are a closed person. You may feel satisfied with the level of intimacy you have established with others, but it's likely that you would benefit from sharing your feelings. Doing so allows others to give you feedback on your ideas and goals, helping you to get a clearer picture of yourself. Begin to change your style by making small disclosures at first. It might be easiest to begin by talking with a friend about your goals.

A score of 18–28: You are average on self-disclosure and have a good balance between your private self and your perceived self.

A score of 29–40: You are very open, but beware. Sometimes indiscriminately opening up can be a sign of personal insecurity, guilt, or a too-strong desire for acceptance by others. If people react to your disclosures with discomfort, it may be that you're revealing more than your listener wants or cares to handle.

EXPLANATION

Studies by Dr. Sidney Jourard at the University of Florida showed that not only are self-disclosures necessary to bring people together, but that they tend to beget self-disclosures from the listener. Thus, a mutual trust begins. Still, it's more of an ideal than a reality to think we can reveal ourselves 100 percent of the time to those close to us. Even in psychoanalysis, where clients are urged to tell everything (Freud's Fundamental Rule), there is resistance to bare all. Research by non-Freudians shows that a silent therapist may be a hindrance to progress. Dr. Everett Shostrom, founder of the Institute for Self-Actualizing Therapy in Santa Ana, California, found that some self-disclosure by a therapist creates a genuine human encounter that speeds up the patient's cure.

It seems that neither extreme of being open or closed is particularly beneficial. It takes good social sense to judge who should or should not be the receiver of our fullest confidence. Nonetheless, it is clear that we must all self-reveal to some extent in order to make meaningful connections with other people—to not do so risks alienation from others, especially those closest to us.

Is Your Romantic Bond Unbreakable?

With marriages occurring at the rate of about two million per year, and divorces or annulments totaling about a third of that number, it's no wonder that psychologists and other experts are giving considerable thought to what makes for wedded bliss or a marital miss. Operating on the notion that "forewarned is forearmed," psychologists have attempted to divine the factors that forecast compatibility and those that betoken a future split. They have learned that among the reasons given in court for divorce, few bear any resemblance to the true reasons for a marital breakdown. A number of expert studies have been conducted in the quest to learn more about what keeps couples together and what tears them apart. Thousands of single and married persons have answered elaborate, lengthy questionnaires designed to predict their chances of maintaining a successful long-term relationship. Having pored over the masses of data, behavioral scientists have finally unearthed what they believe to be the markers of possible future romantic incompatibility.

TEST

The following quiz measures your ability to spot the warning signs of breakup and divorce. Rate each statement "True" if you think it is a significant romantic-bond breaker, and "False" if you do not think it's significant.

1. Age difference of ten years or more between partners.

True   False

2. Significant difference in religious background.

True   False

3. Heavy and varied dating experience by either or both partners before marriage.

True   False

4. High education level (some college) for both spouses.

True   False

5. A strong attachment to parents by either spouse before marriage.

True   False

6. Virginity before marriage.

True   False

7. Both partners were under 21 when married.

True   False

8. An unemployed spouse who feels he or she doesn't get enough money for him or herself and the children.

True   False

9. The husband establishes himself as the dominant personality.

True   False

10. One spouse does not desire children.

True   False

SCORING

To tally your score, give yourself 1 point for each response that matches yours.

1. *False* **2.** *False* **3.** *True* **4.** *False* **5.** *False* **6.** *True* **7.** *True* **8.** *True* **9.** *False* **10.** *True*

A score of 8–10 points: Your marriage is strong. But don't stop there. Keep pleasing each other as you have done to keep it that way.

A score of 4–7 points: You have as solid a bond as most others do. Continue to seek new ways to make it even stronger, for unforeseen adversities may test it.

A score of 0–3 points: Your marriage needs more closeness and stability. Work out your differences, possible disagreements, and unexpressed gripes. Perhaps a counselor would help.

EXPLANATION

1. *False.* In three independent studies, psychologists L. Terman, E. Burgess, and L. Cottrell concluded that even if age differences between spouses are considerably larger than average, this factor is not related to unhappiness and divorce to any important degree.

2. *False.* Studies by psychologist H. Locke failed to reveal that religious differences are a major source of divorce. Apparently, differences great enough to disrupt a marriage are generally great enough to prevent it from occurring in the first place.

3. *False.* In research conducted with more than five hundred couples, there was less need for marital adjustment among those couples who had had many steady relationships prior to marriage.

4. *False.* Partners with a high level of education generally have better marriages and fewer divorces than those who have lower levels of education.

5. *False.* Perhaps contrary to popular assumption, studies have found that the chances of divorce decrease if partners had close ties to their parents when they were single.

6. *True.* Exhaustive work by L. Terman at Stanford University and A. Kinsey at the Indiana Institute for Sex Research demonstrated that the chances of having a lasting marriage are somewhat better if individuals have sexual experience prior to marriage.

7. *True.* The bulk of divorces, more than 50 percent, occurs between partners who are under twenty-one years old. There are six times as many occurrences of divorce among couples who are under twenty-one than among those who are over thirty-one years of age.

8. *True.* Consistent findings indicate that poor family economics is a major cause of divorce. In fact, non-support is the number-one stated cause in divorce courts.

9. *False.* There is abundant evidence that a marriage is more successful and less divorce-prone if the husband is not more dominant than the wife or only somewhat so.

10. *True.* There is considerable evidence that disagreement between partners about wanting children leads to marital disruption. It is surprising how often this crucial point is not thrashed out before marriage.

Can You Read Love Signals?—Part 1

It was evolutionist Charles Darwin who first wrote about the shoulder-shrugging gesture as a universal signal of human uncertainty. Since then the study of non-verbal behavior has revealed many important insights into how body language unwittingly conveys our feelings about each other.

What could be a more fertile field for non-verbal–communication sleuths than that of courtship—the time when, as poets remind us, friendship beckons and love lies nascent?

When boy meets girl a subtle but essential ritual of acquaintance begins, often with scarcely a word said. *Love Signals,* a book by research anthropologist Dr. David B. Givens, deals with the unspoken rituals of flirtation, courtship, and seduction and reveals more than 150 body language cues that disclose sexual attraction or aversion. The following quiz is adapted from his book.

TEST

Love is, without a doubt, the most positive of all human emotions. It ensures the future of civilization. But the capacity to respond to love that is extended to us varies greatly from one person to another. To assess your ability to read the signs, take the following quiz.

1. The voice of someone who is flirting is usually pitched a little higher than usual.

True   False

2. To attract a man, a woman should dress to stimulate his or her sense of touch.

True   False

3. Clothing that is asymmetrical—perhaps it contains a diagonal stripe, or is worn off the shoulder—works to catch the eye.

True   False

4. The quickest way to get to know a person is to:

a. Go dancing   *b.* Go bowling   *c.* Go for a drive

5. You can tell that someone is interested in you if he/she:

a. Stands pigeon-toed   *b.* Tilts his/her head sideways   *c.* Grasps at parts of his/her body   *d.* Does all of these things

6. A woman sitting next to a man on a sofa shifts her weight after he shifts his and raises her glass when he raises his. The moment is right to start a conversation.

True   False

7. On a first date you should show someone you like them by showering them with affection, or casually slinging your arm across their shoulder.

True   False

8. In deciding where to dine, you should consider the interior mood of a restaurant more carefully than its menu.

True   False

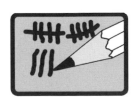

SCORING

People often wonder if there is a particular signal that shows if someone is truly interested in them. Dr. Givens explains that the one strong positive indicator is the "meek cue." It is common among children and involves automatic motions like head tilting, raising of the shoulders, and pigeon toeing. In courtship, the "meek cue" is a sign of submission that gives the other person implicit permission to approach.

To tally your score, give yourself 1 point for each response that matches yours. An item-by-item explanation follows.

1. *True* **2.** *False* **3.** *True* **4.** *c* **5.** *d* **6.** *True* **7.** *False* **8.** *True*

A score of 6–8 points: You have a good sense of signaling in the courtship game and should have no trouble attracting someone or discerning if they're interested in you.

A score of 3–5 points: You should do as well as the average person—some hits, some misses.

A score of 0–2 points: Your signals are crossed. You may be sending the wrong messages and at the same time missing subtle cues that are aimed at you. Some reading on the subject should help. Begin by reviewing the items in this quiz.

EXPLANATION

1. *True.* Flirting produces some tension in the body, including the throat. Tense vocal chords cause the voice to rise in pitch.

2. *False.* A woman should focus on stirring a man's visual senses rather than his sense of touch. Men tend to be quite receptive to their sense of sight.

3. *True.* The first goal of courtship is to capture someone's attention. If your outfit is asymmetrical, it will attract the eye far more effectively than if it were not.

4. *c.* On a drive the pressure is off both parties, and both the car's interior and the passing scenery function as distractions. This creates a less threatening atmosphere and allows for more spontaneous, natural reactions.

5. *d.* All of these signals indicate a submissive, conciliatory demeanor. They reflect a person who is open to interaction.

6. *True.* When someone "mirrors" your actions it is a signal that he is probably ready to communicate with you.

7. *False.* Although certain behaviors like hand-holding will show someone you like them, you may want to wait until you know each other better. Engaging in such "possessive" behaviors in a casual way may be interpreted as forcing a level of intimacy that should develop naturally over time.

8. *True.* The romantic setting of a bistro, for example, stimulates positive feelings. It will be remembered long after the memory of whether the food was good or not.

Can You Read Love Signals?—Part 2

D r. David B. Givens takes a Sherlock Holmesian view of the many unspoken rituals of meeting, dating, and mating that couples use to develop a relationship. Givens observed hundreds of men and women in public places in order to define the various stages of courtship that indicate attraction or avoidance between partners. From the blush of an earlobe to the angle of the toes, men and women unwittingly telegraph their feelings about each other and, says Givens, "There's no hiding love signals, once you know what to look for."

TEST

How well do you send and receive courtship signals? Is it hard for you to tell if someone really likes you? To determine how well you pick up the signs, take the following quiz.

1. If you gaze downward while speaking to an attractive person, you're saying in effect:

a. I'm harmless, you may approach **b.** *I'd rather not speak with you* **c.** *I feel a bit inferior*

2. To present the best possible image, a man should raise his chin, square his shoulders, and slightly lift his chest.

True   False

3. A woman smiles at a man across a hors d' oeuvre table and notices that his lips tense. Is lip-clenching a positive or negative sign?

Positive   Negative

4. When a man sitting next to a woman on a bus reads his magazine a bit conspicuously—overdoes it, mouths the words, chuckles aloud—he's trying to "break the ice."

True   False

5. A sure sign of attraction is when a woman:

a. Points with her index finger **b.** *Rolls her hand, palms up* **c.** *Makes a series of palm-down sweeps*

6. You can tell if a man is flirting with a woman if he keeps checking her reaction to his signals with his eyes.

True   False

7. You can easily spot a "mated" pair because they stand closer than unmatched pairs and touch at will.

True   False

8. The perfect courting outfit consists of which of the following:

a. A three-color contrast **b.** *A tan-colored scarf or tie to accent the flesh tones of your face*

SCORING

To tally your score, give yourself 1 point for each response that matches yours.

1. *a* **2.** *False* **3.** Negative **4.** *True* **5.** *b* **6.** *True* **7.** *True* **8.** *a*

A score of 6–8 points: You have keen insight in deciphering what makes for a courtship.

A score of 3–5 points: You rank average on the love-signal-detection scale.

A score of 0–2 points: Wake up! Love signals may be soaring over your head. Study the quiz items and read up on the subject.

EXPLANATION

1. *c.* A downward glance is a signal of compliance and usually means you are non-threatening and approachable.

2. *False.* This posture conveys a heavy macho image. This could reflect rigidity and self-centeredness. It is better for a man to be gentle and natural.

3. Negative. Lip-clenching indicates an overall tightening of the body. It is a defensive and guarded signal.

4. *True.* These are all subtle signs of reaching out to get the attention of the other person.

5. *b.* A palms-up gesture signals an "I don't know attitude" and a gentleness and readiness to receive direction.

6. *True.* When wooing someone, people do a lot of monitoring. They use it to gauge how effective they are as they approach their target.

7. *True.* Mated couples are long past the stage of keeping "proper" psychological distance. They show intimacy, physical closeness, and body contacts.

8. *a.* Color stirs feelings. A three-color contrast is a potent attractant. If possible, use a pastel accent like a handkerchief or scarf. Pastels are soothing and gentle.

Remember, if you receive negative signals from someone, don't assume that you've failed to attract them. A negative clue could mean that the person isn't ready for you just yet. Maybe he or she is annoyed about something else. Return in a few minutes, if possible, and try again. Your target must be tested a few times. Then, if you still get negative cues, move on.

Can You Read Love Signals?—Part 3

Boy meets girl is the oldest tale in history. The courtship drama occurs in all societies, human and otherwise, and has a vocabulary—both silent and spoken—all its own. We transmit physical signals to show interest in or aversion to others. Behaviors like head tilting, lip tightening, and hair twirling are all courtship cues that can be found throughout the world.

The following quiz is based on researchers' observations of hundreds of men and women interacting in a variety of settings. Based on their studies, psychologists have determined the subtle signals we send that bring us together and break us apart. Anyone can benefit from knowing how to both read and, in turn, send interpersonal signals that can make or break a relationship.

TEST

To learn how well you know the essentials of courtship signals, take the following quiz. Then read the explanations that follow.

1. Someone who flirts is often somewhat excited and childlike.
True   False

2. If a man wants to attract a woman, he should dress in visually stimulating clothing.
True   False

3. Even after having sexual relations, a couple can "keep it casual" if they are mature about their relationship.
True   False

4. When a man swaggers into a party, he is communicating, in effect:
a. "I am here."   *b.* "I am male."   *c.* "I am macho."

5. You should memorize a few "opening lines" in order to make small talk easier at parties.
True   False

6. Most men don't like a woman to wear perfume.
True   False

7. When you wear a "courting outfit," be sure your top is one color and your bottom another.
True   False

8. Women are generally attracted to men who:
a. Are tall   *b.* Are muscular   *c.* Have attractive eyes

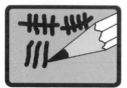

SCORING

To tally your score, give yourself 1 point for each response that matches yours.

1. *True* **2.** *False* **3.** *False* **4.** *a* **5.** *False* **6.** *False* **7.** *True* **8.** *c*

A score of 6–8 points: You have a good sense of courtship signaling and shouldn't have any trouble attracting a partner.

A score of 3–5 points: You are average in the art of love signals, but there is always room for improvement.

A score of 0–2 points: You're missing Cupid's arrow by a large margin. You may be naïve, fearful of involvement, or feel undeserving of closeness.

EXPLANATION

1. *True.* Flirting is a playful activity that often brings out regressive and even somewhat fanciful behavior. It involves an element of daring along with the risk of rejection, and it raises our sense of excitement.

2. *False.* According to research, a man should dress to arouse a woman's sense of touch. In our society, it is more permissible for a woman to touch a man at a first meeting than vice versa. A man should wear clothes with interesting or pleasing textures to stimulate a woman's tactile sense.

3. *False.* Sex provokes powerful emotions, and more often than not, it is difficult to remain emotionally uninvolved when courtship reaches the sexual stage.

4. *a.* The first stage of courting is to draw attention to oneself. Whether it's the swagger in a man or the wiggle in a woman, the aim is to lure a potential target into noticing that one exists and is eager to get acquainted.

5. *False.* Formula opening lines often sound stiff and artificial. It's better to say hello as soon as possible in order to establish a "verbal link." Later, it will be easier to pick up the conversation.

6. *False.* Scents are important attractants for both sexes. But a man can delight in a woman's natural body fragrance just as much as he would her perfume.

7. *True.* Clothing is a key lure in the first stage of courtship (see item 4). You will be noticed more if you wear pleasing contrasts of light and dark colors than if you dress all in one hue.

8. *c.* To a woman, muscles are not as irresistibly fascinating as men assume they are. Rather, "the eyes have it," and many women look for attractive eyes as one important factor in judging whether they like a man's appearance or not.

Remember, the most important factor in your ability to send love signals is being yourself. In the long run, you want someone who's going to like you for who you really are. Love signals are only lures to unite people for mutual discovery. As you navigate through the courtship process, remember that the most attractive thing you have going for you is *you*.

Do You Understand the Opposite Sex?

There's the joke about a young man who describes his ideal bride: "Studies show that people with opposite traits make the best marriages … that's why I'm looking for an attractive girl with money."

The old adage does indeed declare that "opposites attract," but behavioral scientists have exposed this cliché for the ruse it really is. For a long time, scientists and love were strangers who had never really met. Love, subjective and complex, has only recently become a topic of scientific research.

But things are changing, and studies at institutions such as Brandeis University and the University of South Carolina have yielded some interesting results. One major finding is that men and women differ in their reactions to falling—and being—in love.

TEST

To learn how much you know about the differences between the way men and women experience love, take the following quiz.

1. Women are more romantic than men.

True   False

2. Women fall in love faster than do men.

True   False

3. Men tend to feel more deeply about being in love than do women.

True   False

4. Women tend to suffer more from a breakup than do men.

True   False

5. When in love, women tend to reveal more of their deepest feelings than do men.

True   False

6. In sexual matters, men take the initiative more often than women.

True   False

7. Women tend to be slower to fall out of love than men.

True   False

8. A woman who plays hard to get will succeed in arousing interest in the men around her.

True   False

SCORING

To tally your score, give yourself 1 point for each "False" response.

A score of 4 points or more: You're in the superior range and are savvy about love. But take caution! Although you know a lot about love, that may not prevent your head from being dominated by your heart when under the influence of this powerful emotion.

A score of 2–3 points: You have an average understanding of love and how the sexes react under its impact.

A score of 0–1 points: You have notions about love that are unrealistic and aren't supported by the facts.

EXPLANATION

1. *False.* Studies in romanticism in courtship show that men tend to be more romantic than women. They are more likely to agree, for example, with statements like: "Love is a many-splendored thing" and "To be truly in love is to be in love forever."

2. *False.* While a professor at Brandeis University, Zick Rubin devised questionnaires about love that have provided a basis for subsequent research. Rubin found that men tend to fall in love faster and out of love more slowly than women.

3. *False.* Women are more likely than men to feel the agony and ecstasy of love. They are more prone to feel "butterflies" in the stomach, giddiness, and as if they are on a cloud. This is verified by actual physiological measurements of their sympathetic nervous systems.

4. *False.* Rubin and others found that men are likely to suffer more from a breakup, probably because they are less apt than women to confide in someone about their emotions.

5. *False.* Men and women differ little in how much they are willing to reveal about themselves in an intimate relationship. They do differ, however, in the kinds of things they say. Men are more willing to reveal their strengths than their weaknesses. Women, on the other hand, tend to withhold their strengths, especially if they perceive those traits as a threat to the men they desire. Women more readily disclose their weaknesses, their fears, and their feelings about others.

6. *False.* Whatever the methods employed, whether subtle or blatant, the evidence shows that the tendency to initiate sex is shared equally by men and women. In fact, cross-cultural studies show that women initiate sexual advances as often as men.

7. *False.* As discussed in the explanation of item 2, men tend to fall out of love more slowly than women.

8. *False.* It's a popular belief that "hard-to-get" women present more of a challenge to men and thereby seem more appealing. But according to researchers, while this may be somewhat true in the earliest stages of a relationship, it doesn't hold up in the long run. In fact, women who consistently keep their distance may unwittingly invoke a boomerang effect, in which men perceive them as everybody's friend but nobody's lover. After a certain point, acting unattainable simply doesn't stimulate romance.

Will You Win the Battle of the Sexes?

The late Frank Sheed once quipped that there are two basic ways to waste time—by reading subway-car advertisements, and by spitting over a bridge. With all due deference to the noted author-publisher, there is probably a third contender in the race to squander seconds: the battle of the sexes.

These feisty contests tend to generate heat rather than shed light. The truth is that neither sex is superior. In fact, marriage experts find that the strengths and weaknesses of men and women complement each other perfectly in this beautiful game of life and love.

TEST

It's likely that if your beliefs were probed, some outlandish notions about the opposite sex would emerge. The following quiz will help you gauge whether your opinions are on target or way off base.

1. If a woman exercised as often and with as much intensity as a man, she would develop muscle strength equal to that of a man.
True   False

2. Women get the blues more often than men do.
True   False

3. The rate of suicide is higher among women than among men.
True   False

4. Men make better hypnosis subjects than women.
True   False

5. Women are shier than men.
True   False

6. Men are better able to detect the motives of others than women are.
True   False

7. Women daydream more often than men.
True   False

8. Fathers are more likely than mothers to physically abuse their children.

True   False

9. Females engage in sexual activity at an earlier age than males do.

True   False

10. In same-sex friendships, men are more helpful to their male friends than women are to their female friends.

True   False

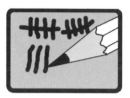

SCORING

To tally your score, give yourself 1 point for each response that matches yours.

1. *False* **2.** *True* **3.** *False* **4.** *False* **5.** *False* **6.** *False* **7.** *False* **8.** *False* **9.** *False* **10.** *False*

A score of 7 points or more: Your insight into the differences between the sexes is good. You have fewer distortions than most people.

A score of 4–6: You have an average degree of understanding of men and women.

A score of 0–3: Chances are you are relying too heavily upon stereotyped notions about the differences between men and women.

EXPLANATION

1. *False.* The male body produces more testosterone than the female body. This hormone adds bulk to muscle fiber, and programs men for larger bones. Men's bodies are 40 percent muscle, compared with 23 percent for women, and exercise won't change this very much.

2. *True.* Women suffer depression more often than men, and are treated for this condition more frequently than men.

3. *False.* The suicide rate is higher among men than women by a ratio of 3 to 1.

4. *False.* Studies show that at any age level females are somewhat more hypnotizable than males.

5. *False.* Shyness is found equally among men and women. Philip Zimbardo, a leading authority on the subject, claims there is no difference between the sexes in shyness.

6. *False.* Generally, women are more aware of social cues than men are. They show more sensitivity than men in picking up such non-verbal messages as body language, facial expression, and tone of voice.

7. *False.* Studies by Jerome Singer at Yale University show that there are very few major differences between men and women in how often and when and where they daydream.

8. *False.* Sociologists summarized several surveys that showed that mothers abuse their children more than fathers do. Mothers were cited as being the abusive parent in 50 to 80 percent of the cases studied, and mothers kill their children about twice as often as fathers do.

9. *False.* Males have sex at a younger age than females do. Once they begin their sexual activity, they engage in sex more often than females. In general, men are more responsive to sexual stimuli and are more likely to engage in self-stimulation than women.

10. *False.* Research done at the University of Utah shows that since women are more self-disclosing, verbal, and affectionate, they tend to have more of a "therapeutic" effect on each other than men have on other men.

How Romantic Are You?

Pink bows, red hearts, candy: These timeless symbols of love remind us that lovers continue to thrive on romance. But if romance could be packaged, it would likely bear the Surgeon General's warning, "This state of mind may be hazardous to your health," for many an ardent lover is dissolved in the bubbly elixir of unbridled infatuation. Romance is indeed a guiding fiction.

Yet according to Drs. Harold K. Fink and E. W. Burgess, who independently studied thousands of couples in love, a relationship requires some romance or else it will dry up. It's a matter of striking a balance between romance and realism that determines whether your love will endure.

TEST

To find out how romantic you really are, take the following quiz, which is based on the work of Fink, Burgess, and other researchers.

1. You had many crushes as a teenager.
True   False

2. You've fallen in love at first sight at least twice.
True   False

3. You feel good when others notice you with an attractive partner.
True   False

4. You usually try harder to be liked when with an attractive member of the opposite sex.
True   False

5. You prefer reading fiction to nonfiction.
True   False

6. At the movies, or reading books, you prefer a love story to comedy.
True   False

7. You enjoy kissing more with your eyes closed.
True   False

8. Your urge for romance is strongest:
a. When the lights are low   b. Any time   c. Only at bedtime

9. During the day, you often think about being intimate with your partner.

True   False

10. You consider it silly when people, middle-aged or older, kiss and hug in public.

True   False

11. You feel a little embarrassed if your partner kisses you on the lips in front of strangers.

True   False

12. You feel uncomfortable seeing a couple kissing passionately in public.

True   False

13. You would feel very upset if you lost an inexpensive but personal gift you got from your partner.

True   False

14. If you give a gift to your partner, it most likely would be flowers, perfume, or cologne rather than a book, CD, or scarf.

True   False

15. You always keep your partner's photo in your purse or wallet.

True   False

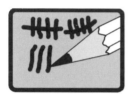

SCORING

Romantics mark items 1 through 7, 9, and 13 through 15 "True," and items 10, 11 and 12 "False." The romantic's answer to item 8 would be "b." To tally your score, give yourself 1 point for each response that matches yours.

A score of 12–15 points: You're a hopeless romantic. You require ample doses of warmth and sentiment. You embroider your fantasies; they titillate you and lift you out of the ordinary. You're the cockeyed optimist of song, a dreamy, maybe impractical idealist, the willing victim of infatuation.

A score of 7–11 points: You are midway between being a romantic and a realist. You can mellow and provide enough romantic sparks when needed. You know where to draw the line between sentiment and good judgment and have probably never been seriously lovesick. Your head may be in the clouds but your feet are on the ground.

A score of 0–6 points: You are a hardheaded realist who sees the world pretty much as it is. No room for fantasy—you're practical to a fault. You might be seen as a cold fish when it comes to amorous notions. You're "thing oriented" rather than "people oriented." You may need to thaw out.

EXPLANATION

In addition to gauging how romantic you are, the questions on this quiz reveal five traits of the romantic person:

Closeness (items 1 and 2): Romantic types usually make attachment to others easily. They readily show their emotions to those they admire. They are easily carried away by sentiment and are blind to the faults of their beloved. They have a strong need to be desired by someone.

Identity (items 3–6): The romantic builds a sense of self-esteem by basking in the glory of those he deems more appealing than himself. The romantic identifies with his lover and derives gratification from her popularity and attention to him.

Fantasy (items 7–9): Romantics have an active fantasy life. They embroider reality for the thrill of it. Often their imaginations take them on a wild gallop. Many times, they seek ideals rather than mates.

Contact Needs (items 10–12): Romantics have strong contact needs. They feel secure when they can be physically near their lover. Sex, affection, and cuddling are important for their self-image. They are not inhibited about making contact with a partner in public or expressing feelings through tender words or actions.

Sentimentality (items 13–15): This trait shows the romantic to be dreamily nostalgic about objects linked to his lover, such as a ring, photos, or song. Such items are imbued with powerful feelings of longing. They symbolize a genuine love attachment to one's partner.

What's Your Intimacy Index?

The search for intimacy is the lonely quest of the human heart. Intimacy is an inborn biological need we first encounter early in life when we are cuddled by our mothers—we never outgrow its powerful lure.

But interpersonal closeness is not as prevalent as you might think. Too often, we learn to adjust to having little meaningful emotional interaction, and it becomes our personalized "love style" to have little or no intimacy at all. This is when the trouble begins.

Studies show that people who are lonely tend to suffer more physical and mental breakdowns than those who are close to someone. Unmarried individuals, compared with those who are married, have higher rates of maladjustment. Children who experience lengthy separations from their parents and family can develop asthma, respiratory disorders, and other diseases, and ill people who fall in love are more likely to recover faster than those who don't. Some experts go so far as to conclude that an intimate love style is just as crucial to a person's well-being as food or water.

Sadly, a world that now rewards uniqueness and independence makes it that much harder to achieve closeness. Many of us are socialized to fend off the attempts of others who try to draw close to us. How intimate would you say you are with the closest person in your life? Are your love styles compatible? Do you ever feel that you are missing a sense of closeness or depth of understanding with your partner?

TEST

The following quiz will help reveal how socially intimate you are. As you answer the questions below, keep in mind your relationship with someone close to you. Perhaps they should also take the quiz.

1. How much of your leisure time do you spend with your partner?

a. Not much   *b.* A little   *c.* A lot

2. How often do you feel it is important for your partner to show you physical affection?

a. Not often   *b.* Sometimes   *c.* Often

3. Would you feel hurt if he/she didn't share deep, intimate feelings with you?

a. Not much   *b.* A little   *c.* Very much

4. Do you understand his/her innermost feelings?

a. Not much   *b.* A little   *c.* Very much

5. How encouraging and supportive are you when your partner is unhappy?

a. Not much   *b.* A little   *c.* Very much

6. How much do you show him/her affection?

a. Not much   *b.* A little   *c.* Very much

7. Do you feel close to your partner?

a. Not much   *b.* A little   *c.* Very much

8. When you disagree strongly, how much does it hurt your relationship?

a. Not much   *b.* A little   *c.* Very much

9. How much time do you spend alone with him/her?

a. Not much   *b.* A little   *c.* A lot

10. How satisfying is your relationship with your partner?

a. Not very satisfying   *b.* Somewhat satisfying *c.* Very satisfying

11. When you quarrel heatedly, does it actually make you physically ill?

a. Not much   *b.* A little   *c.* Very much

12. Do your arguments last two days or longer?

a. Often   *b.* Sometimes   *c.* Not often

SCORING

To tally your score, give yourself 1 point for each "a" response, 2 points for each "b" response, and 3 points for each "c" response.

A score of 27 points or less: Your intimacy level with your partner is fairly low. This may not necessarily mean that either of you is displeased. Both of your closeness needs may be low, and you may be suited to each other. However, if a low scorer is unhappy, it might mean that he/she has difficulty achieving intimacy, and counseling should be sought.

A score of 28–32 points: You have an average degree of intimacy in your relationship compared with other couples.

A score of 33 points or more: You have an intensely close relationship. One thing to be aware of is that you might be too sensitive to each other's feelings and easily hurt when ignored.

EXPLANATION

The quiz is based on social-intimacy research conducted by R.S. Miller and H.M. Lefcourt of the University of Waterloo, Ontario, who tested hundreds of single and married couples. Should you conclude that marriage will take care of all of your intimacy needs, be aware that this is not necessarily the case. Although marriage might seem like an appropriate way to increase a couple's closeness, it can be destructive if a couple has incompatible love styles. In fact, studies show that unhappily married couples who take the quiz come out with low intimacy scores.

Can You Spot the Signs of a Healthy Marriage?

Believe it or not, of the 2 million marriages to be performed this year, about one-third will end in divorce or annulment. Compare this with only about 7 percent of all marriages in 1900! And while many married couples split, it's estimated that about 30 percent remain together—unhappily.

Indeed, marrying the right person and maintaining a honeymoon romance is no easy matter. Even if glaring incompatibilities exist, not even the wisdom of Solomon could persuade lovers lost in a white heat to abandon their plans to tie the nuptial knot. So, if you or someone you know is in love and about to take the plunge, the following quiz might help to predict how things will work out.

TEST

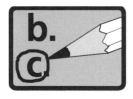

Take the following quiz to find out if your upcoming nuptials are going to end up in a knot or a tangle.

1. We will have courted for less than six months before we marry.
True   False

2. We are both over 21 years of age.
True   False

3. We have many mutual friends of both sexes.
True   False

4. One of us does not desire children, so we won't have kids.
True   False

5. There's a big difference in our levels of education (for example, one of us has gone to college, the other has not.)

True False

6. We are both religious.

True False

7. Our parents and friends heartily approve of our marriage.

True False

8. We are both free of sex hang-ups.

True False

9. Our income will be enough to live on without outside help.

True False

10. We have broken off temporarily three or more times.

True False

11. We are close to each of our parents.

True False

12. When we were young, we were both popular among our peers.

True False

13. Within both our families combined (including siblings, uncles, aunts, etc.), there are fewer than one in twenty divorces.

True False

14. We both get along well with our intended mother-in-law and father-in-law.

True False

15. When we were young, we both generally showed obedience toward significant adults, such as parents, relatives, and teachers.

True False

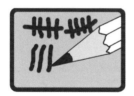

SCORING

To tally your score, give yourself 1 point for each response that matches yours.

1. *False* **2.** *True* **3.** *True* **4.** *False* **5.** *False* **6.** *True* **7.** *True* **8.** *True* **9.** *True* **10.** *False* **11.** *True* **12.** *True* **13.** *True* **14.** *True* **15.** *True*

A score of 12–15 points: You understand the challenges involved in making a marriage work—your chances for marital bliss are good.

A score of 7–11 points: You have an average grasp of what it takes to make wedded life work.

A score of 0–6 points: You may have an overly romantic, and therefore unrealistic, view of what a successful marriage requires. A score in this range doesn't necessarily predict failure, but it indicates that both you and your partner will have to work hard at your relationship in order to keep it healthy.

EXPLANATION

Here is an item-by-item explanation of the quiz.

1. *False.* Long courtships usually make for long marriages. Most marital discord occurs between those who wed before really getting to know each other well.

2. *True.* Studies show that age (and as an offshoot, maturity) plays a significant role in a marriage's success. The rate of divorce is about 50 percent among those who are under twenty years of age.

3. *True.* Having many mutual friends creates multiple ties between lovers and, hence, increases their chances of staying together.

4. *False.* It's best if both partners agree on whether or not to have children before they get married. Although one partner may be willing to accommodate to the other's wishes early on, resentment may build up if that partner's desire to have children persists or strengthens yet remains unfulfilled.

5. *False.* The wider the gap between educational levels, the greater the chance of differences in interests and intelligence, and therefore, the greater the likelihood of a mismatch.

6. *True.* Couples who are religiously active (especially if they practice the same faith) are more likely to have a successful marriage than those who are not.

7. *True.* Peer approval of one's spouse does correlate with success in marriage.

8. *True.* Sexual hang-ups are not the most hazardous pitfalls between people in love, but they can often cause serious disagreements between partners if there isn't enough understanding or a mutual desire to confront the situation.

9. *True.* Financial strain is the leading cause of divorce.

10. *False.* Couples who cannot resolve their differences in ways other than to separate for a while are those most likely to end up in a final split.

11. *True.* Bonding with parents has proven to correlate highly with marriage stability.

12. *True.* Acceptance by stable peers also points to future marital success.

13. *True.* Divorces tend to run in families where it is seen as a viable solution to marital discord.

14. *True.* The ability to get along with and relate to your in-laws is a positive sign—friction with in-laws has proven to be a bad influence on marriage.

15. *True.* Being flexible enough to accept direction from elders is a positive trait. It shows willingness to accept direction from someone we love.

Until recently, behavioral scientists shied away from love as a topic of serious investigation. Traditionally, love was left to philosophers to reason out and explain. But today, important information about the contributing factors to marital rupture can be quickly gathered through the data provided by numerous marriage clinics and counseling centers.

The quiz items are based on extensive work by marriage researchers in the field, such as psychologists Lewis Terman, formerly of Stanford University in California; William Goode, formerly of Case Western Reserve University in Ohio; and others. One study of more than 1,000 couples found that the above-mentioned factors are significant indicators of success or failure in marriage.

CHAPTER 3

A Happy Home

"She's in the bathtub with Mr. Jenkins right now."

Are You Parent Perfect?

D r. Bruno Bettelheim, founder of the Orthogenic School for Children in Chicago (which educates children with behavioral or emotional challenges), stressed that love alone is not enough to raise an emotionally healthy child. Even the most loving parents make mistakes that can adversely affect their children. These are errors of judgment, not of affection.

A wise parent shapes children to respond in acceptable ways by giving love and attention to them when they are good and dishing out consequences when they are not. But there are often vast differences between what any given parent considers acceptable behavior. Though it is ultimately up to individual parents to decide how to raise their children, there are some general guidelines that, when followed, help ensure a child's mental and emotional well-being.

TEST

The following quiz is based on work conducted by James V. McConnell at the University of Michigan who researched mother-child relationships. If you are a parent (or hope to be one), this test can help you determine what misconceptions you might have about healthy parenting.

1. A child should know up front what the punishment will be if he or she misbehaves.
True   False

2. My feelings of closeness for my children are influenced by their behavior from moment to moment.
True   False

3. I feel uncomfortable discussing "touchy" subjects like sex, tobacco, and alcohol with my children when they raise questions about these things.
True   False

4. I regularly take the time to discuss issues with each of my children individually.
True   False

5. It is healthy to show feelings honestly, so it doesn't bother me to praise or scold my child in front of his or her siblings or friends.
True   False

6. Children should be given a sense of independence as soon as possible, even if it means they might suffer painful defeats now and then.
True   False

7. I rarely discuss controversial subjects with my children, because it might cause arguments.
True   False

8. I show my children that I'm on their wavelength and very much like one of their peers.
True   False

9. Children shouldn't be allowed to question their parents' judgments.

True   False

10. Basically, most children really want their parents to give them more freedom than they have.

True   False

11. If I make demands of achievement too early in life, it will create too much anxiety in my child.

True   False

12. Young kids who are hard to manage usually need more discipline.

True   False

SCORING

To tally your score, give yourself 1 point for each response that matches yours.

1. *False* **2.** *False* **3.** *False* **4.** *True* **5.** *False* **6.** *False* **7.** *False* **8.** *False*
9. *False* **10.** *False* **11.** *False* **12.** *False*

A score of 10 or more points: You are a savvy parent and are doing a good job of parenting. Keep reading and asking questions.

A score of 5–9 points: You fall in the average range of most parents. But don't stop there. Keep seeking new ways to improve your child's healthy development.

A score of 0–4 points: Though you are undoubtedly a loving parent, you may have some brushing up to do. Review the explanations and discuss them with another parent whose judgment you respect, or perhaps even a professional. You might also consider joining a parent's group to find ways to strengthen your parental role and form a more nurturing, positive relationship with your child.

EXPLANATION

1. *False.* It's better not to lay down the law before a child has actually erred. Try to let children know that you don't approve of certain behaviors, but avoid casting the threat of reprisal before they act out.

2. *False.* It might be hard to feel love when frustrated with a naughty child. But part of the art of parenting is to show disapproval while at the same time projecting an implicit feeling of love for the disobedient child.

3. *False.* Children are naturally curious as they try to make sense of the world around them, and should be free to ask questions of their older, wiser parents. It is the insecure parent who labels a subject "taboo," then proceeds to avoid it. Even if you are uncomfortable discussing an issue, something constructive should be said in response to a child's question.

4. *True.* Each child deserves special time alone with his or her parents. The wise parent respects a child's individuality, and recognizes that each may have particular needs and pose unique questions about life.

5. *False.* Although honesty is important, generally children should not be scolded in front of others.

6. *False.* Granting independence is a constructive gesture, but it's not always in a child's best interest. Occasionally independence, especially in decision making, can be granted too readily, and this is often indicative of a parent's own weakness or indecisiveness. Before freedom is allowed, be reasonably certain that no pronounced harm will come to your child.

7. *False.* Arguments can be constructive if they are fair and generate more light than heat. Good parents use conflicts and the subsequent discussions to enlighten children on important issues.

8. *False.* It's a mistake to abandon your role as parent for the sake of convincing your children that you can relate to them. A child should not feel that you are like his or her peers. There are other ways to show empathy without relinquishing your authority role—such as sharing fun times and making joint decisions.

9. *False.* Parents who allow their kids to pose sincere questions about their decisions tend to raise self-reliant and responsible children. By allowing your child to respectfully question your authority, you show not only that you are confident in your choices, but that you respect your child.

10. *False.* In a poll of some 27,000 pupils, the National Institute of Student Opinion found that 66 percent wanted their parents to be somewhat strict with them, compared with 33 percent who wanted less discipline.

11. *False.* Research by Harvard University psychologists shows that the earlier the parental demand for reasonable achievement, the stronger the subsequent drive for achievement, provided the child has a good relationship with his parents.

12. *False.* Although fair discipline is necessary, much of the difficulty might be corrected by a more perceptive parent. Work at the University of Wisconsin showed that mothers who described their toddlers as "difficult" were often the mothers who displayed low awareness of a distressed infant's needs when reviewed on a videotape. The study found that these parents required more help in developing sensitivity to their child's needs.

Can You Spot a Troubled Child?

"Since Sammy has been in Ms. Hamway's class, he is doing better. She seems to sense when something is bothering him and knows how to help him." A mother recently told me this, and it raised a question: Why do kids respond better to some teachers than to others?

Children are sensitive to how a teacher judges their behavior. A teacher's attitude—what the teacher believes to be "good" or "bad" behavior—can have a bearing on the development of the personality of a pupil. A classic study done more than fifty years ago found that there were great incongruities between how teachers and conservative parents defined "serious" behavior problems and how child experts did.

Could you be out of step with the experts' opinions? Are you aware of the most predictive signs of maladjustment in your child, or are you focusing on relatively unimportant behavior your child will probably outgrow?

TEST

An opinion survey asked teachers, parents, and child psychology experts to rank certain behaviors as indicators of future maladjustment. The ten behaviors listed below were included in the survey. To take this quiz, rank the behaviors in terms of their relative seriousness, with "1" being extremely serious and "10" being not serious—place your rankings in the column marked "Your response." Then move on to the "Scoring" section to see how well you can spot a troubled child.

Your response	Experts	Difference	
_____	_____	_____	Unsocial, withdrawn
_____	_____	_____	Suspicious
_____	_____	_____	Unhappy, depressed
_____	_____	_____	Resentful
_____	_____	_____	Fearful
_____	_____	_____	Cruel
_____	_____	_____	Easily discouraged
_____	_____	_____	Suggestible
_____	_____	_____	Overly-critical of others
_____	_____	_____	Sensitive

Your score _____

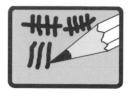

SCORING

The behavior patterns you just ranked were taken from a list of fifty characteristics rated by child psychologists, psychiatrists, social workers, and counselors. The order in which the items appear concurs with the manner in which they were ranked, with "unsocial" being the most problematic behavior a child can exhibit. To tally your score, write the numbers "1" through "10" down the "Experts" column, beginning with "1" in the first row and ending with "10" in the last. This will give you the specialists' rankings. Then, for each item, calculate the difference between your ranking and that of the experts and place that number in the "Difference" column. Add up all the numbers in the "Difference" column—the sum of the numbers is your score. The lowest possible score is 0 and the highest is 50. A score of 25 is the average between these extremes. The closer your score is to 0, the more you agree with child experts about what constitutes serious deviant behavior.

EXPLANATION

Unfortunately, adults who are responsible for healthy mental outlooks in kids are often oblivious to the most important signals of trouble ahead. All ten behaviors in our quiz are, to some degree, serious reflections of something wrong in the child, but those that fall among the first three or four ranks are the most serious. In all fairness, it must be said that what teachers consider to be a serious problem is an action which upsets the teacher, the school, and the classroom routines, not necessarily that which behaviorists consider a predictor of neurosis.

When other studies using the traits above were repeated some thirty years later, the findings showed that the ratings of teachers and parents had shifted and become more similar to the experts' opinions. But the experts themselves also became more conservative in their judgments. Current surveys show that all three groups are now more concerned with behavior like withdrawal, unhappiness, depression, and fearfulness. The most encouraging result of these studies is that, compared with their predecessors fifty years ago, more highly trained teachers and better informed parents are beginning to focus on deviant patterns before they get out of hand.

Are You a Guilt-Free Working Mom?

Today, more than half of all families with children under the age of six have a working mother. In 1973, that figure was one-third. With increased job competition and costs of living, the number of double-paycheck families is expected to rise even more in the next decade. Along with other societal changes, the working mother has been blamed for a variety of family problems.

Some argue that teenage delinquency, alcohol abuse, and high occurrences of school dropouts are largely the result of the mother's absence from the day-to-day life of her children. Others maintain that the amount of time a mother spends away from home is not as crucial as the quality of the time she spends when she's there.

TEST

Where do you weigh in on this issue? Would you feel confident asserting the position that a woman's choice to pursue a career should not have her feeling guilty about her family life? Take the following quiz to find out.

1. A mother should not work full-time while she has a child under the age of five.
a. Disagree   *b. Disagree somewhat*
c. Agree somewhat   *d. Agree completely*

2. A husband should not be expected to look after a baby if his wife is at home.
a. Disagree   *b. Disagree somewhat*
c. Agree somewhat   *d. Agree completely*

3. A mother's most important job is to raise her children.
a. Disagree   *b. Disagree somewhat*
c. Agree somewhat   *d. Agree completely*

4. It is difficult for a mother to reach the top of her career without her family suffering.
a. Disagree   *b. Disagree somewhat*
c. Agree somewhat   *d. Agree completely*

5. If a child is ill, it's better if the mother, rather than the father, takes time off from work to care for the child.
a. Disagree   *b. Disagree somewhat*
c. Agree somewhat   *d. Agree completely*

6. If it became necessary, a mother should be prepared to quit her job to look after her kids until they are old enough to go to school.
a. Disagree   *b. Disagree somewhat*
c. Agree somewhat   *d. Agree completely*

7. It is difficult for a woman to balance being a good wife and mother if she has a demanding job.
a. Disagree   *b. Disagree somewhat*
c. Agree somewhat   *d. Agree completely*

8. Children grow up better under their mother's care than under their father's.
a. Disagree   *b. Disagree somewhat*
c. Agree somewhat   *d. Agree completely*

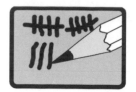

SCORING

To tally your score, give yourself 1 point for each "a" response, 2 points for each "b" response, 3 points for each "c" response, and 4 points for each "d" response.

A score of 28 points or more: You are strongly conservative and have traditional values about men and women. To you, fathers are important but mothers are the most essential part of the home scene; you believe families shouldn't share moms with the business world.

A score of 24–27 points: Your views are middle of the road. You would agree that a mother's first responsibility is in raising her children, but believe that this can be balanced with her career goals.

A score of 23 points or less: Your views regarding a mother's role are liberal. You believe she should have the chance to fulfill her own career goals while she raises a family.

EXPLANATION

Whether you have traditional attitudes about a mother's family role depends largely on your own parents' relationship. A broad study of family patterns conducted at Cornell University by Dr. Hazel L. Ingersoll showed that men raised in a home where father was boss and mother stayed home also tended to play the dominant role when they married. A woman will also tend to be dominant if her mother was dominant. No matter who plays the role of breadwinner, if the atmosphere is congenial, the children will accept that arrangement as normal and tend to imitate it when they marry.

During the 1960s, many people adopted liberal attitudes about what a partner's ideal family role should be. Even Dr. Benjamin Spock, labeled a male chauvinist by feminists, recanted his belief that "women will always play a major role in child care, and mother, not father, must give up whatever career time necessary to care for small children." The famed pediatrician later conceded that neither spouse need be a dominant personality to foster a happy family environment. Undoubtedly, whether a woman chooses to remain at home or to work at promoting her career, her children will be well-adjusted so long as she is a caring, attentive mother.

Are You Tuned in to Teens?

A poet once said, "Childhood shows the man as morning shows the day." It's a pithy line that reflects a basic truth—kids show early signs of the adults they will become. But all too often we parents get so caught up in the rush of life that we don't take the time to notice what's influencing our kids' attitudes and actions. Do we still think about teens in terms of the old clichés?

TEST

How adept are you at assessing the attitudes of teenagers? Do you understand how and why they develop and grow in a particular direction? The following quiz should show you how teen-savvy you are.

1. Most kids want their parents to be more permissive.
True   False

2. If you hold strong political views, your children will tend to rebel with views contrary to yours.
True   False

3. In this age of liberation, youths form opinions more or less independently of their parents' influence.
True   False

4. Children are born with an innate capacity to love their parents.
True   False

5. Your job will affect how you treat your kids.
True   False

6. Your son will become a social achiever if he has a father with a strong personality.
True   False

7. Offspring of ambitious executives almost always stand a good chance of advancing in work when they mature.
True   False

8. The more a youngster is involved with his parents rather than with his peers, the more likely he will move up the social ladder later on.
True   False

9. Children from large families tend to be more self-confident and friendly than those from smaller families.
True   False

10. Since he or she has the advantage of learning from others, the youngest in a family tends to be brighter than the oldest.
True   False

SCORING

To tally your score, give yourself 1 point for each response that matches yours.

1. *False* **2.** *False* **3.** *False* **4.** *False* **5.** *True* **6.** *False* **7.** *False* **8.** *True*
9. *False* **10.** *False*

A score of at least 4 indicates that you have an adequate understanding of the various factors that influence the behavior and development of teenagers.

EXPLANATION

Here is an item-by-item explanation of the quiz.

1. *False.* In a poll of some 27,000 high school students, the National Institute of Student Opinion found that two-thirds of students wished their parents would be somewhat strict with them, compared with just one-third who wanted "to be left alone" (free of discipline) most of the time.

2. *False.* This is true for only a small proportion of youngsters. A large study of U.S. college students found that youths tend to become either more conservative or more liberal than their parents, especially if they are more educated than their parents. But relatively few take an extreme political stand against their parents.

3. *False.* The vast majority of youngsters' opinions, attitudes, and beliefs are handed down by their parents. For example, nearly three-quarters of all voters vote for the party their parents chose. Parental influence on values can last a lifetime.

4. *False.* Love for either parent is not innately determined. Love is acquired. A youngster learns to love those who love him as expressed through their actions, especially concrete ones, such as providing care, giving affection, and supplying food.

5. *True.* Parents unconsciously teach kids behavior they have been rewarded for at work. For example, studies show that a parent who is independently creative will encourage his or her children to be independent. But if he or she succeeds at work by taking direction from others, that parent will tend to teach his or her children to be obedient and follow orders.

6. *False.* In his book *American Class Structure*, sociologist Joseph Kahl indicates that it's more important for the mother, rather than the father, to have a strong personality. A son is much more likely to become a social climber if his mother, rather than his father, has a strong personality. Actually, the combination that most often produces an upwardly mobile son is a dominant mother and a less dominant (or even passive) father.

7. *False.* Psychologists A. Sostek and S. Sherman of Boston studied male executives and found that fathers who were strongly dominant at work often carried that habit home. In general, their parenting style was more autocratic than participatory, and their children were more likely to build up feelings of resentment. As young adults, these children tended to avoid responsibility and were more likely to develop problems with authority figures at work.

8. *True.* Sociologist Joseph Kahl found that in a large number of cases, kids who spend considerable time with their parents were more socially successful than those who associated more often with their peers. Studies have also found that the smaller your family, the greater the chance your teenager will be a social striver.

9. *False.* Two studies conducted by Ross Stagner at Wayne State University in Michigan showed that there is a distinct tendency for kids from smaller families to be more well-adjusted emotionally, although the differences are not overwhelmingly great. In large families, parents have to try harder to give support to all their children.

10. *False.* Psychologist Robert Zajonc did an analysis of some 400,000 adolescents at the University of Michigan and demonstrated that, in general, IQs decrease from first to last born.

Do You Have Parental Burnout?

Here's a help-wanted ad you won't see in your local paper: Seeking woman with energy, willing to work twenty-four hours a day. Must be patient, loving, wise, dependable, and organized. Must be able to cook, sew, shop, clean, and quickly learn new methods necessary for keeping a household happy and cared for. Salary: none.

There'd be no takers for a job like that, right? Wrong! Today there are 60 million mothers who tackle such tasks seven days a week. Furthermore, every year 3 million more apply for the position.

If you're a mother, you understand the rigors of this job like no one else. And surely you're aware of its rich rewards. But sometimes you might feel that your labor output exceeds your job benefits. Do you ever feel that you are being taken for granted?

TEST

The following quiz was designed to gauge the stress level that mothers are feeling on the job. If you're a mother, take the quiz to see how close to burnout you really are. If you're not a mom, put yourself in your mother's shoes and answer the questions as you think she would answer them.

1. Lately, do you feel more fatigued than usual?
a. Often *b.* Sometimes *c.* Rarely

2. Do you have difficulty laughing at jokes your family makes about you?
a. Often *b.* Sometimes *c.* Rarely

3. Are you bothered by physical complaints, such as aches, cramps, pains, and headaches?
a. Often *b.* Sometimes *c.* Rarely

4. Do you feel irritable and quick-tempered?
a. Often *b.* Sometimes *c.* Rarely

5. Are you forgetful about dates and appointments, or do you lose or misplace personal belonging?
a. Often *b.* Sometimes *c.* Rarely

6. Are you seeing less of your close friends and loved ones?
a. Often *b.* Sometimes *c.* Rarely

7. Do you experience sleeplessness?
a. Often *b.* Sometimes *c.* Rarely

8. Do you ever feel inattentive to the needs of others?
a. Often *b.* Sometimes *c.* Rarely

9. Are you easily distractible and unable to concentrate?
a. Often *b.* Sometimes *c.* Rarely

10. Are you careless about the appearance of your home?
a. Often *b.* Sometimes *c.* Rarely

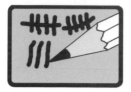

SCORING

To tally your score, give yourself 3 points for each "a" response, 2 points for each "b" response, and 1 point for each "c" response. Read on for explanations of your (or your mother's) stress level.

A score of 10–16 points: You are a veritable pillar of stability. You can withstand the pressures of day-to-day living and still function at peak efficiency in your job.

A score of 17–23 points: You are in the average range. You handle the job stress fairly well and are not in danger of burnout. But you will need continued recognition of your hard work in order to maintain morale.

A score of 24–30 points: You are showing signs of early burnout. You need more staff, more time off, and daily incentives (like more love, hugs, and praise) to get back to normal. Express your needs to your family, and don't be afraid to ask for help.

EXPLANATION

As time passes, most mothers assume an all-giving role with their families. This behavior has been studied by psychologists Dorothy Juneward and Dru Scott at the Transactional Analysis Management Institute of San Francisco. They found that some time after the first child arrives, many mothers adopt this pattern. Here are some of the warning signs: A mom feels she must, at all times, and in all places, be a supermother. She devotes most of her time and energy to her husband and children and little to herself. She has a problem accepting her deserved pleasures. She feels guilty when she relaxes, has fun with misgiving, and buys personal things only after much shopping around.

And as if such self-denial isn't enough, this type usually develops into the family scavenger, finishing the wilted lettuce, munching bread ends, and selecting wings when the family dinner is roast chicken. If this sounds all too familiar, the mother in your family may be in a rut. She's grown accustomed to her place.

We've heard much recently about burnout striking down even the most hardy of our business executives, but nary a word about mothers. If burnout really does exist in the work world, then those unsung heroines of the kitchen and the car pool deserve a screening, too.

Dr. Herbert Freudenberger, in his book *Burnout*, explains that this creeping malaise can attack families in much the same way that it affects business executives. So take the time to evaluate the mother in your family. Does she have enough job satisfaction? Does she need more vacation time? Are the benefits worth enough? And most of all, monitor her behavior for signs of burnout. If you see them, perhaps it's time to give her an end-of-year bonus (love, hugs, praise) a bit earlier—and more often.

CHAPTER 4

Social Senses

"It's of a personal nature."

Do You Cause a Spark or Leave No Mark?

The personality we project is a kind of visual résumé for all to see and evaluate. But we may be completely oblivious to how others truly see us. We'd never know the truth about the image we project unless friends and relatives gave us their honest opinions. But, for the sake of preserving feelings, would they *really* level with us? Your social image is an elusive portrait. It can be estimated only indirectly by getting feedback from others or observing how people react to you.

TEST

How well can you read the signals showing what others think of you? Is the image you project out of line with the real you? The following quiz should help to provide some answers. Review the items below and rate each according to how adequately you think it describes you.

1. Casual acquaintances forget things about me, such as what I do and where I live.
a. Often   *b.* Sometimes   *c.* Rarely

2. People tease me about personal traits such as my interests, beliefs, the way I dress, etc.
a. Often   *b.* Sometimes   *c.* Rarely

3. People fail to introduce me to those nearby.
a. Often   *b.* Sometimes   *c.* Rarely

4. Sales clerks and waiters tend to be inattentive to me or wait on me last.
a. Often   *b.* Sometimes   *c.* Rarely

5. At a gathering, strangers forget my name after the introductions, although they recall the names of others they just met.
a. Often   *b.* Sometimes   *c.* Rarely

6. In group conversations, my opinions or ideas are not asked for.
a. Often   *b.* Sometimes   *c.* Rarely

7. People often interrupt me, and act as though their ideas are more important than mine.
a. Often   *b.* Sometimes   *c.* Rarely

8. In public places, my companions ask me to alter my behavior, i.e., to hold doors, watch my table manners, or lower my voice.
a. Often   *b.* Sometimes   *c.* Rarely

9. Others sometimes explain things to me in a simplistic manner, as if I were naïve.
a. Often   *b.* Sometimes   *c.* Rarely

10. People chide me for raising topics at inappropriate times or places.
a. Often   *b.* Sometimes   *c.* Rarely

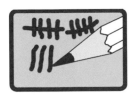

SCORING

To tally your score, give yourself 1 point for each "a" response, 2 points for each "b" response, and 3 points for each "c" response. Refer to the scores below to see how strong your social image is. (Remember, this is not who you are, but who others believe you to be.)

A score of 25–30 points: You project a strong social image. Others remember important details about your life, and are likely to address you first in a group setting and listen carefully to your ideas and opinions. You are most likely a charismatic, popular person.

A score of 17–24 points: You project an average social image. People are generally happy to see you and include you in their groups, although you don't always make the strongest first impression. But you rarely exhibit offensive or antisocial behavior, either. Most people fall into this category.

A score of 10–16 points: You may need to work on your social image. Review your answers with a trusted friend, and ask for honest suggestions on how you might try to act differently with people to bring your image in line with how you really feel on the inside. Everyone has the ability to improve his or her social image, so don't feel frustrated if you fall into this category.

EXPLANATION

To see ourselves as others see us, as the Scottish poet Robert Burns one wrote, is a rare gift. When we fail to pick up on how others see us, it is often because we want to preserve the image of ourselves that we have in our own mind.

There are three components that comprise our personal portrait: our self-image (who we think we are), our projected image (the person we try to show to others), and our social image (how we are viewed by others). Our social image is the topic of this quiz.

Studies by Dr. Carl Rogers, founder of the Center for the Study of the Human Person in La Jolla, California, have shown that the more these three images concur, the more emotionally stable we are. It's rare, however, that the three conform exactly. Sometimes, because only one or two of our traits are revealed, others with a narrow mindset may get a distorted picture. When a person focuses on a general trait like our race, nationality, or religion, our social image may be tainted by their stereotyped perceptions. Generalizing about someone on the basis of one or two obvious traits is called a "halo effect," and it may present a good or bad overall impression.

According to this quiz, those who are unimpressed by our social image will reveal it indirectly; for example, they will mispronounce our name, neglect us, or treat us as if we are immature or inadequate. They may betray a limited respect for our ideas, impose upon us an informality that breeds contempt, be generally unmindful of our presence, or try to dominate us.

How we look, act, and speak often invites specific reactions from others. If we appear nervous and non-authoritative, chances are we'll be treated that way. If we act hostile, we'll invite attack. If, on the other hand, we project self-confidence, we'll probably garner respect. As much as we may hate to acknowledge this simple truth, our social image is an important predictor of our success in life.

Are You a Con Artist in Disguise?

At some time or another, we've all been in a position to persuade others. Whether it's a child who beguiles his parents for another cookie or a wily con artist who bilks the innocent out of their hard-earned money, both behaviors require a certain degree of shrewdness.

In their work at Columbia University in New York, psychologists Charles Turner, Daniel Martinez, and Richard Christie independently probed the personal characteristics that mark a person for either social or professional success. Several factors came to the fore: IQ, education level, school achievements, social background, and the personality of one's parents. But the investigators learned that it's not these traits alone that predict success. As a matter of fact, these traits account for only 65 percent, at most, of one's success in the business world. The other 35 percent is attributable to a personality factor loosely defined as getting others to do what you want.

TEST

Whether you're at the top of the success ladder, struggling midway, or angling for a toehold on that first rung, the following quiz will help reveal whether, unwittingly or not, you rely on manipulation to get ahead.

1. There is nothing wrong with telling a white lie in order to avoid hassles.
True   False

2. It is probably shrewd to flatter important people who are in a position to help you.
True   False

3. As a child, I was known as a bully.
True   False

4. In this strongly competitive world, most anything short of being unethical is justified in getting ahead.
True   False

5. Most successful people lead clean, honest lives.
True   False

6. P. T. Barnum was right when he said, "there's a sucker born every minute."
True   False

7. It is not possible to abide by all the rules and still get ahead in this world.
True   False

8. Most people are brave.
True   False

9. The biggest difference between law violators and others is that the violators were not smart enough to avoid being caught.
True   False

10. Don't tell anyone your real reason for doing something unless it is useful to do so.
True   False

SCORING

The quiz was adapted from the work of professors Turner and Martinez. For want of a better term, the quiz measures your "manipulativeness," or Machiavellian tendencies (the explanation section gives more information about Machiavelli.). To tally your score, give yourself 1 point for each response that matches yours.

1. *True* **2.** *True* **3.** *True* **4.** *True* **5.** *False* **6.** *True* **7.** *True* **8.** *False* **9.** *True* **10.** *True*

A score of 3 points or less: You are a low Machiavellian and tend to be more than willing to entertain another person's viewpoint. You are a harmonizer and, at times, may be even too submissive in carrying through your own ideas and goals.

A score of 4–6 points: You are average when it comes to conning others. You are likely to push your ideas moderately, but not to the point of overruling or manipulating others.

A score of 7 points or more: You are a high Mach. You do not share traditional notions about social rights and wrongs. You are an independent thinker who dislikes conforming to your peers. According to the researchers at Columbia, you are cool and at times even distant. You might sometimes treat others as objects. If this is you, it might be time for a change. Your score on the quiz "How Empathic Are You?" (page 90) should be another indicator of this trait.

EXPLANATION

The term "Machiavellian" is derived from the military, government, and business tactics proposed by Niccolo Machiavelli, an influential politician-writer of the 16th century. As counsel to royalty, he advocated the use of cunning and contrivance when needed to assure one's political goals. Compared to his other ideas, these amoral aspects of his doctrines have always attracted the greatest attention, yet he also devised brilliant strategies to make Italy a free republic. Nonetheless, his name is equated with power and manipulation.

You don't have to be smart to be Machiavellian. Manipulative tendencies do not correlate with IQ, as many might believe. Both bright and dull people can be high Mach types. The difference is that the bright high Mach types are more likely to succeed, while those less crafty can't conceal their motives as readily. High Machs tend to be credible and charming, with an action-oriented message. Their easiest target is a person with low IQ and little self-esteem who is taken by surprise by the ruse. High Machs succeed mostly when their prey is distracted or indecisive. Body language experts tell us not to look for shifty eyes as a sign of insincerity. Those who are experienced at deception actually have a steadier gaze than those who are honest. Also, it is not true that "con artist" drives go hand in hand with psychopathology; many normal people use power tactics because they work for them.

Manipulativeness is probably learned from our parents. This is confirmed by Dr. F. Geis and Richard Christie in their book, *Studies in Machiavellianism.* In homes where parents are high Machs, the child who escapes this influence is likely to be the first-born, who often develops traits diametrically opposed to the tactics of his or her canny parents. And although Machs are found among both sexes, studies show that men are more manipulative than women.

Are You Socially Anxious or Socially Secure?

Comedian Robin Williams once said that even with all his years of performing, he still gets nervous when facing a new audience. Social anxiety is a burden everybody endures, from childhood through old age. Many never shake it no matter how hard they try, though some of us have learned to disguise it quite well.

When unusual or special social situations arise, how high is your social angst? Take the following quiz to find out. You may also want to ask someone who knows you well to respond to the items as he or she thinks you might answer. When you're both finished, compare results.

TEST

This quiz will help you evaluate whether you simply have sweaty palms or if you suffer from social anxiety. Rate how tense or uncomfortable you would feel under the following conditions.

1. Being approached by a policeman.
a. Not tense at all   *b. Slightly tense*   *c. Quite tense*

2. In a casual get-together with acquaintances and co-workers.
a. Not tense at all   *b. Slightly tense*   *c. Quite tense*

3. When sitting with a group of strangers in the waiting room at the doctor's office.
a. Not tense at all   *b. Slightly tense*   *c. Quite tense*

4. Talking to your boss about a raise or a teacher about your grade.
a. Not tense at all   *b. Slightly tense*   *c. Quite tense*

5. Speaking to an attractive person of the opposite sex whom you've just met at a cocktail party.
a. Not tense at all   *b. Slightly tense*   *c. Quite tense*

6. Talking sweetly to your lover over the phone with strangers nearby.
a. Not tense at all   *b. Slightly tense*   *c. Quite tense*

7. Being interviewed for an important job.
a. Not tense at all   *b. Slightly tense*   *c. Quite tense*

8. Arguing about politics, ethics, or other non-personal issues among your friends.
a. Not tense at all   *b. Slightly tense*   *c. Quite tense*

9. Being in a new group where you are the only one of your race, nationality, or religious background.

a. Not tense at all   *b. Slightly tense*   *c. Quite tense*

10. Meeting a friend by chance while shopping for something personal and potentially "embarrassing," such as underwear, feminine products, or condoms.

a. Not tense at all   *b. Slightly tense*   *c. Quite tense*

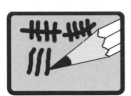

SCORING

To tally your score, give yourself 1 point for each "a" response, 2 points for each "b" response, and 3 points for each "c" response. To determine your level of social unease, refer to the scores below.

A score of 24–30 points: You are very anxious socially and probably too worried about what others will think of you. Too much concern about your impact on others might indicate personal insecurity or a sagging self-image.

A score of 18–24 points: You have an adequate amount of social sensitivity to what others look for and expect from you. You feel accepted by others and are satisfied enough with your social image to function passably well in new social circumstances.

A score of 10-17 points: You are quite self-assured and very relaxed when around others. You may even be oblivious to how they view you. Your self-image is shaped by your own internal standards and very little by what society may judge as acceptable behavior.

EXPLANATION

According to research by Mark Leary at Denison University, one of the greatest difficulties in studying social anxiety is that it is manifested in two distinct ways: a person's self-report (what our quiz measures), and actual behavior, as demonstrated by withdrawal, speaking in a low voice, and being passive.

The quandary is that one may feel socially anxious but also be good at covering it up. People with these characteristics—labeled "shy extraverts" by Dr. Philip Zimbardo of Stanford University—have learned to appear sociable and relaxed while feeling awkward. Research shows that the less self-esteem we have, the more likely we are to experience anxiety in the presence of others.

This finding is also backed up by the work of Professors R. E. Glasgow and H. Arkowitz conducted at the University of Oregon, who found that people with high social anxiety tend to date little. The main reason underlying their reluctance is their poor self-perception. These types would score low on the quiz and are often called "avoidant personalities" because they are acutely sensitive to humiliation and deprecation by others and actively avoid people in order to protect themselves. Social angst is actually a fairly prevalent problem in our culture, and as a result, a number of shyness clinics have formed to help people learn to feel more comfortable in their own skin.

Can You Read Body Language?

The next time you chuckle at the antics of a comedic duo performing a slapstick routine, you'll notice that two roles are being played. One person gets the pies in the face, while the other throws them. Most relationships, curiously enough, are like this. One partner is dominant while the other is submissive. We reveal which role we play in various ways, the most obvious of which is through speech. Phrases like, "I'm very sorry," "Excuse my clumsiness," or "May I please?" all imply a degree of submissiveness. Phrases like, "Can you do such and such?" "Will you let me know?" or "Get back to me soon" all reveal the dominant mode.

However, dominant or submissive behavior isn't shown only through what we say. It can be conveyed non-verbally as well. Can you tell the difference between these roles just by watching two people interact? If you know what to look for, body movements contain signs that are just as telling as words, but not nearly as obvious.

TEST

Following is a list of everyday gestures. To learn how well you can decipher these physical flags, rate each behavior as dominant or submissive.

1. Shoulder shrugging
Dominant   Submissive

2. Touching of partner
Dominant   Submissive

3. Smiling
Dominant   Submissive

4. Interrupting a partner's speech
Dominant   Submissive

5. Gazing downward
Dominant   Submissive

6. Jerking of head sideways
Dominant   Submissive

7. Putting a hand on one's own body
Dominant   Submissive

8. Gestures with palms down
Dominant   Submissive

9. Tilting head to the side
Dominant   Submissive

10. Loud, low-pitched voice
Dominant   Submissive

11. Very soft voice
Dominant   Submissive

12. Fingers spread and pointed toward partner
Dominant   Submissive

13. Rotating palms upward
Dominant   Submissive

14. Sped up speech
Dominant   Submissive

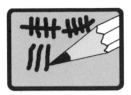

SCORING

All the even-numbered items are "Dominant"; the rest are "Submissive." To tally your score, give yourself 1 point for each response that matches yours.

A score of 4 points or less: You are missing important body cues that may reveal the attitudes of others.

A score of 5–8 points: You have an average understanding of dominant and submissive body gestures.

A score of 7 points or more: You have an above-average sensitivity to non-verbal cues.

EXPLANATION

Psychologists have long-relied on "expressive movements," or body cues, to probe the inner feelings of people. Today, kinesics, the study of body movements, is a natural outgrowth of this practice. Numerous pop manuals on body language promise to teach people how to read others by presenting a laundry list of postures and definitions of what each movement means. But such popular books are not always reliable.

What little we know for sure about body language comes from careful research done by people like anthropologist Dr. David Givens and the late psychiatrist Albert Scheflen. The items in our quiz are taken from their studies. Gestures of dominant persons are usually directed outwardly to another person. A steady unwavering gaze or the touching of one's partner is a dominant action. Submissive gestures are usually protective, such as touching one's own body or shrugging one's shoulders.

Unfortunately, submissiveness is equated with inadequacy. But this is not necessarily so. Submissive people are often happy, well-adjusted, and productive. Furthermore, one isn't always submissive in every situation and with all people. More likely, a person displays degrees of dominance and submissiveness at different times depending upon the setting. Assuming a role that is proper in a given situation, of course, is a sign of maturity.

Could You Break the Law?

The sober reality of human nature is that we all have the capacity to be saints or sinners. Through socialization, a child is taught what is and is not considered acceptable behavior. But despite the best intentions of parents and schools, there are still some who go wrong.

Although relatively few of us have the tendencies of hardened criminals, we sometimes bend the law. Jaywalking, speeding, and gambling may not be enough to put one behind bars, but, if committing illegal acts becomes a substitute for our perceived deprivations, the growing habit of such behavior just might eventually develop into an antisocial lifestyle.

If you've ever wondered about the strength of your inner discipline against illegal tendencies, you are not alone. Most of us occasionally wonder: "Is there a Mr. Hyde in me?" The question is: Why do some of us resist temptation while others succumb to it? One answer is that it depends on our inner psychological make-up. When the seed of temptation falls on soil that is ready to sustain it, it's likely to flower.

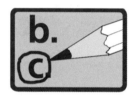

TEST

Below is a list of traits that experts have found to be typical of consistent law violators. The list is based on a sixteen-year study of some 240 male offenders.

1. I am highly sensitive when rebuffed or put down by someone.
True   False

2. I am chronically angry, upset, and frustrated.
True   False

3. I have gone through very low periods where I have felt utterly worthless.
True   False

4. I am, or have yearned to be, on my own— free and independent of people and the restraints of society.
True   False

5. Compared with others, my need to do risky things to find excitement is high.
True   False

6. I have had episodes of boundless optimism that exceeded the reality of my situation.
True   False

7. I often have done or craved to do things that are forbidden by society.
True   False

8. As a youngster, I often got my way by bluffing, bullying, or using physical force.
True   False

9. As a teen, I often committed petty, illegal acts like shoplifting, driving too fast, or cheating on exams.
True   False

10. I lose my temper easily.
True   False

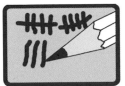

SCORING

To tally your score, give yourself 1 point for each time you responded "True." Read on to discover your criminal potential.

A score of 0–3 points: Not only are you a pillar of civic obedience, you also have good inner control of your alien impulses. It's unlikely you'll ever seriously break the law.

A score of 4–7 points: You're average in your capacity to be law-abiding. Occasionally, you take a chance and break a law, but it's probably nothing more than a misdemeanor.

A score of 8-10 points: You have more than your share of the traits that are found among those who act anti-socially. You might want to ask yourself why you keep going against the rules. You might even consider counseling to look into this issue further.

EXPLANATION

The search for personality characteristics that will predict crime is not new. For some 400 years, criminal offenders have been the subject of intense investigation. Traditional conclusions have been that such violators of the law are victims of limiting circumstances like broken homes, poverty, and unemployment. But more recent studies by psychologists S. Yochelson and S. Samnow strongly indicate that these are not the only causal factors, for most persons raised in such limiting circumstances are law-abiding.

Rather, researchers have concluded that disordered thinking and faulty attitudes are the most significant contributors to illegal behavior. These include reactions like feelings of persecution, being hypercritical of others, and notions of grandiosity. In a two-volume work called *The Criminal Personality*, researchers identified the fifty-two most common traits of criminal offenders. Our quiz contains ten of these traits.

Are You a Fair-Weather Friend or a Friend for Life?

Learning to forge lasting relationships is a perennial topic on the bestseller list. And the books seem to draw the same conclusions: As creatures of habit, we live best when linked to others in some meaningful way.

Finding friends in a hurried world isn't easy. But when you get down to it, it's not a matter of finding a friend as much as it is a matter of being one. What we do, say, and think about others can either help or hurt our ties with them.

 **TEST**

Take the following quiz to learn whether you have the qualities that make for a solid friendship.

1. My friends seldom seek my advice on personal matters.
True   False

2. It usually takes a long while for me to forgive someone who has offended me.
True   False

3. I have often been described as touchy and oversensitive.
True   False

4. I belong to at least one volunteer group (civic, religious, etc.)
True   False

5. I would never become the business partner of a personal friend.
True   False

6. I agree that when the chips are down, most friends will put their own interests ahead of yours.
True   False

7. I'm more cautious than most people in relying on the judgment of others.
True   False

8. I feel uncomfortable when a friend entrusts me with a secret.
True   False

9. I often find it hard to confide my intimate feelings to friends.
True   False

10. I can become so absorbed in my own projects that I sometimes don't miss losing contact with intimate friends.
True   False

11. I become annoyed, more so than most others, when a boss gives me an order.
True   False

12. I don't think I would continue to befriend someone who associated with an enemy of mine.
True   False

SCORING

To tally your score, give yourself 1 point for each response that matches yours.

1. *False* **2.** *False* **3.** *False* **4.** *True* **5.** *False* **6.** *False* **7.** *False* **8.** *False*
9. *False* **10.** *False* **11.** *False* **12.** *False*

A score of 9–12 points: You are probably a very good friend. You show a caring and trusting attitude toward others. You would extend a hand of friendship before it is offered to you.

A score of 5–8 points: You have average capacity to be a good friend to others. For the most part, you are happy with your friends, but you continue to seek others who will enhance your life.

A score of 0–4 points: You have difficulty keeping friends. You have a subjective view of people, which hinders you from giving yourself to them. You might want to ask yourself, "Am I really happy?" If your answer is no, start on a self-improvement program now!

EXPLANATION

Here is an item-by-item explanation of the quiz.

1. *False.* If friends don't seek your advice on personal matters, it's likely you're sending signals to them that you're not interested in the nitty gritty of their lives. You're probably transmitting "distance producing cues," which we send to those with whom we want only a limited friendship.

2. *False.* Work done by California psychologist J. P. Guildford confirms that those who hold grudges are generally unfriendly. When we harbor resentment, it blocks the open expression of constructive feelings toward others.

3. *False.* On the whole, touchy and oversensitive persons will find it hard to blend their attitudes with those of others. As a consequence, they learn to get by with only a few friends in their lives.

4. *True.* People who join groups have above-average friendship instincts. They seek out such groups so that these drives can be expressed. In such settings members satisfy each other's affiliative needs.

5. *False.* It depends very much on the individuals involved. There are times when it is not only wise but necessary to go into a business venture with someone personally close to you. In most successful partnerships there is a trust, sharing, and mutual respect—all basic ingredients of friendship.

6. and **7.** *False.* Both of these items relate to trust. Dr. Philip Zimbardo, an expert on the friendship process, has found that those who can't accept outside viewpoints usually develop a distrust of others at an early age. For most of their lives, they have difficulty in making and keeping friends.

8. and **9.** *False.* Items 8 and 9 relate to the work of Professor Sidney Jourard, author of *The Transparent Self.* He found that there can be no real sense of closeness between two persons without self-disclosure by each. Likewise, when we feel awkward about sharing a secret with someone, we are revealing that we prefer to keep them at a psychological arms-length and don't want them to be close friends.

10. *False.* This question is often found in personality tests. A "true" answer is more likely given by one with low social interests or one who finds making friends a chore.

11. *False.* There's a connection between our attitudes toward authority and our ability to be friendly. Researchers have found that people who resent authority figures usually find it difficult to be friendly with their peers.

12. *False.* It may be a touchy balancing act, but the mark of a mature friend is one who can be close to people who are in disagreement with each other. You're in for disappointment if you define "friend" as one who dislikes the same people you do.

How Empathic Are You?

An actor came to me for help in playing an important role. The director of his play was dissatisfied because the actor was unable to convey a strong enough sense of sadness in his role as a grief-stricken man. The actor, whose own life circumstances were similar to those of his character, was blocked in his effort to feel empathy for the man he was meant to portray.

Empathy is a distinctly human ability to feel the emotions of someone else. If you grew jittery the last time you watched James Bond clutching the edge of a rooftop in a movie, that's empathy. But it's also broader than that.

Empathy is a special form of identification. It is a term coined by Sigmund Freud to describe how we see ourselves in someone else and make their experiences and attitudes part of our own self-concept. Social psychologist Kimball Young summed it up nicely: "The image of the self could not arise without some degree of sympathetic identification of the young child with others."

Often we don't understand someone's troubles because we haven't lived through them ourselves. Or, if we have experienced similar difficulties, they caused such pain that our empathy has become blocked. Such was the case of the actor mentioned above: He wouldn't allow himself to feel deep sorrow for fear it would revive depressing memories of his dying mother.

Empathy is an essential trait for dealing with others and much research has been conducted to understand it. At Eastern Illinois University, Dr. Mark Davis skillfully constructed tests that measure empathy. His findings, which appeared in the *Journal of Personality,* have important implications for understanding social development. The following quiz is adapted from his work.

TEST

To learn how you compare with others in your ability to empathize, choose the answer that best corresponds to how you would feel in each situation below.

1. In emergencies, I become emotional.
a. Not at all   *b.* Somewhat   *c.* A good deal
d. Very much   *e.* Exactly

2. Even when I'm pretty sure I'm right, I'm patient enough to listen to other people's arguments.
a. Not at all   *b.* Somewhat   *c.* A good deal
d. Very much   *e.* Exactly

3. I feel deeply for the characters in tearjerker movies.
a. Not at all   *b.* Somewhat   *c.* A good deal
d. Very much   *e.* Exactly

4. When I am with a depressed person, I become uncomfortable and it is difficult for me to talk.
a. Not at all   *b.* Somewhat   *c.* A good deal
d. Very much   *e.* Exactly

5. I feel uneasy when someone I know casually tells me about a personal problem.
a. Not at all   *b.* Somewhat   *c.* A good deal
d. Very much   *e.* Exactly

6. When a disagreement with someone becomes intense, I can't deal with it at the time.
a. Not at all   *b.* Somewhat   *c.* A good deal
d. Very much   *e.* Exactly

7. Others have said that I am soft-hearted.
a. Not at all   *b.* Somewhat   *c.* A good deal
d. Very much   *e.* Exactly

8. I daydream about things (good and bad) that might happen to me.
a. Not at all   *b.* Somewhat   *c.* A good deal
d. Very much   *e.* Exactly

9. The true answer to the great majority of issues is not clearly black or white—usually the truth is somewhere in between.
a. Not at all   *b.* Somewhat   *c.* A good deal
d. Very much   *e.* Exactly

10. I feel sad when I see a lonely stranger in a group.
a. Not at all   *b.* Somewhat   *c.* A good deal
d. Very much   *e.* Exactly

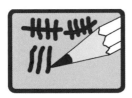

SCORING

Women are consistently found to be more empathic than men. So, on average, women will receive scores that are at least 2 points higher than those of their male friends.

To tally your score, give yourself 0 points for each "a" response, 1 point for each "b" response, 2 points for each "c" response, 3 points for each "d" response, and 4 points for each "e" response. Keeping in mind that our quiz is not a perfect gauge of empathy, read on to find out what your score suggests.

A score of 25–40 points: Your empathy level is high. You are able to understand how others feel and offer them your support in a considerate manner.

A score of 12–24 points: You have an average level of empathy. You can be made to understand how someone else is feeling, but you don't always sense it right away.

A score of 0–11 points: You exhibit low levels of empathy. You find it hard to identify with others, and can't relate to how they are feeling unless you are in a similar situation.

EXPLANATION

There are four basic ways in which we show empathy:

1. Through fantasies and reactions to fictional characters (as in items 3 and 8 of the quiz).

2. Through concern for others (items 5 and 10). Empathizers readily resonate the feelings of those having bad times.

3. Through a shift in perspective (items 2 and 9). Even though they may disagree, empathizers are flexible enough to entertain another person's point of view.

4. Through distress (item 1). Empathizers are generally sensitive, and tend to experience strong emotions in upsetting situations.

Empathy is a form of caring and interest in others. It starts early in life through imitation. By the age of two months, an infant begins to mimic others' smiles and this empathic identification expands in ever-widening circles to include other people and social contexts. The depth of our empathy depends upon how much empathy we received and learned from others as we grew up. However, the capacity for empathy doesn't peak in childhood. The ability to feel for others can increase with age and experience.

Resonating with the feelings of others is necessary for the survival of all cultures. Freud's disciple, psychoanalyst Alfred Adler, called it "fellow feeling." Without it, all social cooperation would be impossible. There is no area of human interaction that escapes its impact.

How Popular Are You?

When Groucho Marx quipped, "I'd never join a club that would have me as a member," it was a funny way of saying that his self-esteem was at zero level. Fortunately, most of us are not in this category and have enough good feelings about ourselves to be reasonably happy. One powerful means of gaining self-esteem is through social acceptance. It's like getting a vote of confidence from others about our value. In a way, others validate our sense of worth.

Psychologists find that those who are popular are "middle-of-the-roaders" who strongly accept the attitudes and ideas of their group; they are not extremists in their thinking. Further, they have the social skills to form mature and lasting relationships with others.

TEST

How popular are you? The following quiz will suggest how well you get along with people and/or if you have the potential to boost your social skills.

1. In the past month, I have received two or more social invitations.
True   False

2. My friends seek my advice about their problems.
True   False

3. When the joke is on me, I usually laugh along with the rest without feeling resentment.
True   False

4. Some friends divulge their intimate secrets to me.
True   False

5. When something is bothering me, I readily turn to friends for help.
True   False

6. I have participated actively in at least two social groups for the past two years.
True   False

7. I usually make friends through people I already know rather than on my own.
True   False

8. I choose to be friendly with someone mostly on the basis of common interests.
True   False

9. I am late for at least one out of three social engagements.
True   False

10. I don't like to be dependent on others and don't encourage others to be dependent on me.
True   False

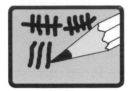

SCORING

To tally your score, give yourself 1 point for each response that matches yours.

1. *True* **2.** *True* **3.** *True* **4.** *True* **5.** *True* **6.** *True* **7.** *False* **8.** *False* **9.** *False* **10.** *False*

Read on to see where you fall on the popularity meter.

A score of 8–10 points: You are, or have the potential to be, above average in popularity and enjoy a wide circle of friends.

A score of 5–7 points: Like most of us, your popularity is solidly in the average range.

A score of 0–4 points: You are more of a private person than the popular type.

EXPLANATION

Research on the topic of popularity is scant, but some facts are known. Popular people tend to attract others and are role models for us to emulate. Often they are leaders. At work, a boss who is popular has strong advantages over one who isn't. His or her workers will show less absenteeism, higher morale, less tension, and more productivity. Popular people tend to be born later in the family lineup. They develop more social skills because they interact with their siblings and others for a longer time.

Disliked boys often compensate by fighting with peers and by bullying them. Girls, on the other hand, sometimes drift into promiscuity in order to be accepted. Dr. Philip Zimbardo has called this "a physical means of achieving an illusion of psychological security."

Other social scientists have shown that children can improve their popularity levels. Third and fourth graders were trained on such things as manners, listening skills, and other social-interaction techniques. Their studies yielded marked results. The children who received training mixed better with their peers, showing more concern, listening more intently when spoken to, and other traits that up one's popularity quotient. On the adult level as well, social interaction is a skill like reading and writing that can be learned through the use of videotapes, talks, and group counseling.

Do You Listen or Leave 'Em Hanging?

They say that listening well is an art form. But do you recall how frustrating it was the last time you spoke with someone who was only partly present? Being an effective listener isn't just about hearing what's said; it also involves conveying your interest and understanding.

Good communication keeps human relations going. But too often there is a breakdown at the receiving end. A prime example would be parents who are at a loss when their teenager "tunes out" during a conversation. Parents don't know what to focus on in the two-way exchange and don't profit enough from the experience. But according to Dr. Thomas Gordon, author of *Parent Effectiveness Training*, parents can break through this impasse and get their children to talk with them by "active listening." The technique can be learned and applied to conversations with adults, too.

TEST

To discover how well you listen, take the following quiz.

1. When my friends have something on their mind, they usually use me as a sounding board.
True   False

2. I don't mind listening to the problems of others.
True   False

3. In a social gathering, I move from one conversation to another, often feeling that there is a better partner across the room.
True   False

4. I grow impatient with someone who doesn't come to the point quickly.
True   False

5. I tend to complete the jokes or stories that others tell.
True   False

6. While people are speaking to me, I find myself thinking of the next thing to say to them.
True   False

7. Most people are boring conversationalists.
True   False

8. I usually do more talking than whomever I am with.
True   False

9. People repeat things once or twice when speaking to me.
True   False

10. I would rather give a talk than hear one.
True   False

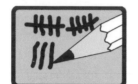

SCORING

To tally your score, give yourself 1 point for each response that matches yours.

1. *True* **2.** *True* **3.** *False* **4.** *False* **5.** *False* **6.** *False* **7.** *False* **8.** *False*

A score of 8 points or more: You are an above-average listener. Friends most likely seek you out when they have a problem they need to discuss, and you are probably popular at social gatherings.

A score of 5–7 points: Your listening skills are average. You are like most people—sometimes you listen very well, and at other times you probably let your mind wander. Remember, there is always room for improvement.

A score of 0–4 points: Frankly, you are not the best listener. You tend to tune out more often than you tune in. Read the "Explanation" section that follows for some tips on how you can improve your skills.

EXPLANATION

Why do trained counselors relate to people better than laymen do? What do these pros do differently to help others to grow? Dr. Gordon calls it "active listening." He has taught this technique to parents who have been "written off" by their children, and has found that it can be used equally well in "adult" arenas such as professional environments and social situations.

Dr. Gordon's method, which he has taught to more than 100,000 parents, is based on the work of Dr. Carl Rogers, founder of client-centered therapy, who taught that active listening focuses sharply on creating empathy, an essential element for good ties with others. Active listening involves entering the private perceptual world of the speaker, seeing things from his or her point of view, and becoming thoroughly at home in it. It means paying attention to the underlying feelings being expressed and not so much to the statements themselves.

For example, if a downcast youngster says: "Won't my friend come over to play with me today?" it would be only partly correct to respond to the content of his remark by replying, "No, he had to go to the dentist." In responding in that way, you are missing his underlying feelings. Using active listening, you would answer something like this: "I know you're disappointed that your friend isn't coming today, but don't feel blue. Let's plan a good time with him for tomorrow." Active listening enables you to immediately get to the heart of what's bothering someone. It demonstrates that you really understand. Granted, it will take a little more time to discover exactly what underlying emotion is being expressed, but it will bring good results in the end.

To train yourself for better listening, take these three steps:

1. Commit yourself to being a better listener.

2. Read up on the subject and practice skills like active listening.

3. Determine what your defective habits may be by studying the quiz items. Hopefully this will get you started on attaining better communication know-how.

How Thoughtful Are You?

Can you recall the good feeling you had when someone carried your bulky package, held a heavy door, or allowed you to cut ahead of a long line? In a world of chaos, favors granted by perfect strangers remind us that social graces are still well and thriving. But we humans are variable creatures, and a host of conditions influence whether or not we will choose to render aid to others. Some mitigating factors include our relationship to the afflicted, our mood, or even the weather. A needy person's age also influences our generosity. In one experiment at the New School for Social Research in New York City, unsuspecting subjects were asked to help various people in distress. Researchers found that elderly persons were helped more readily than those who were middle-aged or younger. Also, the study showed that it's more likely we'd come to the aid of a woman than a man, to a woman who is pretty than one who is plain, or to one who is well-dressed, compared with one who is sloppy in appearance.

Then there are the other, more subtle facilitators or inhibitors that bring out the best or worst in us. If we have a good self-image and if we perceive ourselves as helpful, it's more likely that we will extend a helping hand. We're less likely to help if others nearby are watching than if we are alone or if there is a high noise level nearby, as on a subway or near a churning lawn mower.

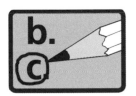

TEST

Below are some questions that will gauge your thoughtfulness. Respond "Yes" or "No" to each one. Be honest!

1. Do you, when instructed, write your account number on your checks when paying bills?

Yes No

2. When you meet someone, do you usually turn so that the sunlight will not be in their eyes?

Yes No

3. When a waiter clears the table, do you readily hand him items that are hard for him to reach?

Yes No

4. When stopping to speak with someone on the street, do you remove your sunglasses?

Yes No

5. After reading the newspaper at home, do you put it back together?

Yes No

6. When picking fruit from a fruit bowl, do you usually take the piece that is about to go bad?

Yes No

7. Do you push your chair in close to the table when leaving a restaurant?

Yes No

8. Do you give your teeth a good scrubbing before you visit the dentist?

Yes No

9. Do you hesitate to take the last appetizer on the platter?

Yes No

10. When you buy a small item, do you often carry it as is, to save the clerk the trouble of wrapping it?

Yes No

11. At the checkout counter, do you turn items so the cashier can see the price or bar code?

Yes No

12. When you dial a wrong number, do you usually hang up without saying anything?

Yes No

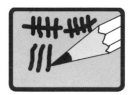

SCORING

To tally your score, give yourself 1 point for each answer that matches yours.

1. *Yes* **2.** *Yes* **3.** *Yes* **4.** *Yes* **5.** *Yes* **6.** *Yes* **7.** *Yes* **8.** *Yes* **9.** *Yes* **10.** *Yes* **11.** *Yes* **12.** *No*

A score of 8 points or more: You have a great willingness to be helpful to others, and don't hesitate to lend a hand when it is needed.

A score of 5–7 points: You rank about average on the trait of thoughtfulness. You will give help if someone asks for it, but don't always think to offer.

A score of 0–4 points: You exhibit little interest in being of help to those who might benefit from it. You may be oblivious to the needs of others. Try to pay more attention to those around you.

EXPLANATION

Doing a good deed is called "social compliance" in psychology, and often the manner in which a favor is asked is crucial to how someone will respond. Researchers have found that people comply more often if the requester states his or her request openly, and if he or she follows it with a plausible reason. When it comes to granting wishes, we are guided by a simple formula: Request plus reason equals greater compliance. This is a good thing to remember. For example, if you asked to cut in line at the grocery store, you'd probably get a better response if you explained that your child is not feeling well and that you would like to get her home quickly. In addition, compliance has a ripple effect. Researchers at Manhattanville College in Purchase, New York, studied shoppers at a department store and found that when requests were accompanied by even such a trifling offering as a warm smile, shoppers tended to be kind and helpful to those nearby.

How responsive you are to the needy is learned behavior instilled by your childhood role models. The National Institute of Mental Health in Washington, D.C., found that some babies as young as one year old are capable of comforting others who are crying or in pain. You can increase your level of thoughtfulness if you encourage yourself to become more conscious of people, and practice daily the niceties that make for smoother interpersonal relationships.

Are You a "Take-Charge" Type?

It seems that whenever two people meet, the issue of who is dominant is the first one to be settled, most often very subtly. Between students, who gets better grades? Between executives, who earns more or has the larger office? Between tomboys, who is tougher? Among animals, the case is clear. Birds, in particular, size each other up and then decide who shall henpeck whom to show superiority.

Dominance-submissiveness is probably the most basic of all interactions between creatures great and small. In Western culture, submissive behavior is not rewarded. We tend to push our children ahead with notions of the "go-getter," and expressions like "Never say die," all of which reflect our belief in the value of personal dominance.

TEST

Where do you stand on the dominant-submissive scale? The following quiz may provide the answer.

1. I could bluff my way past a guard without feeling uneasy.

True   False

2. I have heckled or sharply questioned a public speaker.

True   False

3. I would feel uneasy about scolding a workman who didn't complete a job I asked him to do.

True   False

4. I would feel timid about starting a conversation with a stranger.

True   False

5. I don't mind the job of introducing people at gatherings.

True   False

6. I can cut into a long line without feeling guilty.

True   False

7. When I drive, it doesn't bother me to follow a long line of cars.

True   False

8. When dining with friends, I would complain if a waiter brought me a somewhat small portion of food.

True   False

9. When I'm at odds with someone, I don't call him or her. I usually wait until he or she calls me first.

True   False

10. I like to instruct people on how to do things.

True   False

SCORING

To tally your score, give yourself 1 point for each response that matches yours.

1. *True* **2.** *True* **3.** *False* **4.** *False* **5.** *True* **6.** *True* **7.** *False* **8.** *True* **9.** *True* **10.** *True*

A score of 0–4 points: You're low on dominance, high on submissiveness. If you enjoy this laid back style of life, great. But if you feel unhappy with the way you often come out in encounters with others, consider getting help to become more assertive. Dominance can be enhanced through assertiveness training, a trend that was kicked off in the 1960s and persists today.

A score of 5–7 points: You have an average balance of dominance and submissive tendencies. You probably respond to different situations on a case-by-case basis, and not with any set type of behavior.

A score of 8–10 points: You are high on dominance. If people accept this in you and follow your lead (many leaders are high dominants), then you should be happy. However, if your high levels of dominance are causing friction in your day-to-day interactions, it may be time to back off, be more empathetic, and let others win some points every now and then, too.

EXPLANATION

One question that has tickled the brains of scientists for years is this: Is a dominant personality inherited or learned? Among animals, it is a strongly inherited trait. Among humans, genes seem to play only a minor role in our levels of boldness or timidity. They are largely patterns learned from family and peers.

Nowhere has the interplay of dominant and submissive roles been studied more than in marriage, the most interdependent of all human partnerships. Here there is almost always one spouse who tips the dominant/submissive scale in his or her favor. But it isn't as totalitarian as it sounds, for as long as mutual love and respect are there, spouses are generally happy to accept their respective roles and feel comfortable in them. At the same time, children usually adopt the attitudes of parents. They copy their parents' role-playing style and accept it as the norm when they themselves marry. Studies of families conducted at Cornell University in New York by Dr. Hazel Ingersoll showed that boys with dominant fathers tended to follow in their fathers' footsteps when they themselves had families. Likewise, if a girl grew up with a timid mother, she would likely fall back on such behavior when handling conflicts, and act accordingly.

An interesting note about dominance has to do with birth order. An only child tends to be dominant among his peers. In homes where there is more than one child, however, dominance is more random among the siblings. Tests show that the strongest, most intelligent people (and animals, too), are usually the ascendant ones in their group. Of course, people aren't always just dominant or just submissive. The role we take depends on a host of factors: the people near us, our relation to them, the mood we're in, the circumstances of the occasion, and what role is expected of us, among others.

CHAPTER 5

On the Job

*"Great news, Bayless! I've worked out the most diabolical fold
for a map you ever saw!"*

How Ambitious Are You?

Martha Stewart, Oprah Winfrey, and Ted Turner are all proven high achievers. If tested, the results would probably show that they have certain personality traits in common: high intelligence, high drive, and a high energy level. But why is it that some of us get ahead while others, with equal potential, don't?

Psychologist David McClelland, formerly of Harvard University, has studied this question extensively. He studied nearly twenty personality traits—including the need for dominance, love, and nurturance— at the Harvard Psychology Clinic. Now, his findings are used worldwide to show managers how to encourage achievement in the workplace.

TEST

Do you have what it takes to be a winner? To learn how high your ambition level is, take the following quiz. It was adapted from the work of Professor McClelland and John Ray, of the University of New South Wales in Australia.

1. I am able to put work out of my mind when off the job.
True   False

2. I very much enjoy betting in football pools, lotteries, races, etc.
True   False

3. You only live once, so a happy life with many friends is more important than the hard work of attaining accomplishments.
True   False

4. I very much dislike seeing things wasted (like food, fuel, paper, etc.).
True   False

5. I make daily lists of things to do.
True   False

6. I would prefer working with a congenial but somewhat inept partner than one who is difficult but highly competent.
True   False

7. I have a tendency to do things today rather than put them off until tomorrow.
True   False

8. I have a strong interest in the lives of successful people.
True   False

9. I am time-conscious about almost everything I do.
True   False

10. I prefer important, difficult tasks that involve a 50 percent chance of failure to those that are less important but easy and more enjoyable.
True   False

SCORING

To tally your score, give yourself 1 point for each response that matches yours.

1. *False*   **2.** *False*   **3.** *False*   **4.** *True*   **5.** *True*   **6.** *False*   **7.** *True*
8. *True*   **9.** *True*   **10.** *True*

A score of 8–10 points: You are intensely ambitious. Your drive to succeed may be highly beneficial, but keep in mind that pushing yourself to extremes could be detrimental to your well-being. It's important that you also take time to relax and enjoy life.

A score of 5–7 points: You have an average level of ambition and can live with limited goals of accomplishment. You're probably content to win some and lose some, as long as you have fun along the way.

A score of 0–4 points: Your ambition level is low. Could you be down in the dumps, insecure about your strengths, or lacking inspiration? Perhaps you're content with the way things are going, but if you are dissatisfied, it might be helpful to talk it over with a trusted friend or trained job counselor.

EXPLANATION

The items in the quiz are very similar to those used in questionnaires designed to measure ambition. People with high levels of ambition tend to answer as follows:

1. *False.* Strivers, because they are highly involved in their work, continue to dwell on business problems long after the workday is over.

2. *False.* Those with high aspirations rarely engage in the magical thinking that success or good fortune will come from forces outside their own abilities and drives.

3. *False.* Winners are willing to work hard at their goals and put their social life second.

4. *True.* Achievers avoid waste in any form and try to keep unnecessary activity at work and play to a minimum.

5. *True.* Good organization and planning are typical of strivers who are time-conscious and, ideally, would like each minute to be a constructive step toward a goal.

6. *False.* Fast-trackers don't agree with this type of partner arrangement. They are willing to sacrifice congeniality for a partner who will help them make it to the top.

7. *True.* Achievers usually have a strong sense of urgency. They keep ahead of deadlines by finishing assignments on time. In general, they are not procrastinators.

8. *True.* Those with strong ambition find role models at the top. If a person does not admire success, he or she is less likely to be highly ambitious.

9. *True.* Most achievers are good planners. They use time in the same manner as they use their personal resources. Wasted time is a lost opportunity to do something constructive.

10. *True.* The key word here is "important." Those who aim high recognize that most people can handle easy tasks, although the easy tasks aren't usually the ones that bring distinction. However, "important" work begets duties that will bring recognition and additional challenges at higher levels.

People who win are self-starters who enjoy taking charge of their own destiny. But not all the traits of ambitious people are obvious. One study of 100 male and female managers in Illinois, for example, showed that high achievers are more involved with community affairs, read more books, are more religiously active, and are more stubborn in the face of difficulties.

Even children who start off life at a disadvantage can grow up to be highly ambitious and successful people. McClelland's book, *The Achieving Society*, discusses this phenomenon. In it, he maintains that bad influences can be overcome even much later in life. Field studies in India, for example, showed that businessmen with low levels of ambition who were coached and encouraged were able to raise their levels of aspiration and improve their business activities to make significant economic gains for their communities.

Keep in mind, however, that ambition is a relative term and that we have largely been discussing it in the context of the workplace. You may find that your sense of success lies elsewhere: in building good relationships with others, developing artistic talent, leading a neighborhood group, or raising a healthy and happy family.

What's Your Work Style?

It takes all types to keep the business world thriving. When experts study various types of workers, they often limit themselves to levels of authority—those who are leaders and those who are followers.

But there are other ways to categorize workers to get a better understanding of their contribution to a company. Professor Michael J. Kirton, in his research at the Hatfield Polytechnic Institute in St. Albans, England, studied the work styles of more than 500 employees. He correlated each worker's style with his or her value in the firm, then classified each of them on the basis of how they tackled job problems and how they felt about work. For the most part, two groups emerged: adapters and innovators. Adapters are the steady performers who carry out daily tasks without fuss. Innovators are those who desire and need change. Indeed, both types complement each other and are vital to company growth.

Reflect on your present or past work situations. You probably haven't thought much about whether you are an adapter or an innovator. Here's a chance to find out where you stand.

TEST

In the following quiz ahead, which is based on Professor Kirton's findings, answer each item as it best describes you.

1. I am precise and methodical in my approach to problems.
3
 a. *Not like me* **b.** *Somewhat unlike me*
 c. *Somewhat like me* **d.** *Very much like me*

2. I can usually tolerate boring jobs.
1
 a. *Not like me* **b.** *Somewhat unlike me*
 c. *Somewhat like me* **d.** *Very much like me*

3. It bothers me to cope with several problems at once.
1
 a. *Not like me* **b.** *Somewhat unlike me*
 c. *Somewhat like me* **d.** *Very much like me*

4. When faced with an assignment, I'm known as a "steady plodder."
3
 a. *Not like me* **b.** *Somewhat unlike me*
 c. *Somewhat like me* **d.** *Very much like me*

5. Compared with others, I am a conformist when it comes to society's general expectations.
1
 a. *Not like me* **b.** *Somewhat unlike me*
 c. *Somewhat like me* **d.** *Very much like me*

6. I make few errors when involved with routine tasks for long periods of time.
1
 a. *Not like me* **b.** *Somewhat unlike me*
 c. *Somewhat like me* **d.** *Very much like me*

7. I stick to tried-and-true solutions to problems.
2
 a. *Not like me* **b.** *Somewhat unlike me*
 c. *Somewhat like me* **d.** *Very much like me*

8. I would prefer to work for a company than to work for myself.
3
 a. *Not like me* **b.** *Somewhat unlike me*
 c. *Somewhat like me* **d.** *Very much like me*

9. I like to work with colleagues who don't "rock the boat" by suggesting changes.
1
 a. *Not like me* **b.** *Somewhat unlike me*
 c. *Somewhat like me* **d.** *Very much like me*

10. I have more patience with detailed work than do most people.
3
 a. *Not like me* **b.** *Somewhat unlike me*
 c. *Somewhat like me* **d.** *Very much like me*

11. It would bother me to act without my boss's permission.
1
 a. *Not like me* **b.** *Somewhat unlike me*
 c. *Somewhat like me* **d.** *Very much like me*

12. I enjoy detailed work.
4
 a. *Not like me* **b.** *Somewhat unlike me*
 c. *Somewhat like me* **d.** *Very much like me*

SCORING

To tally your score, give yourself 1 point for each "a" response, 2 points for each "b" response, 3 points for each "c" response, and 4 points for each "d" response.

A score of 34–48 points: You are a highly adaptive worker. You follow guidelines and get the job done well.

A score of 22–33 points: You strike a balance between being an adapter and an innovator.

A score of 10–21 points: You are a highly innovative worker. You like to modify, adjust, and reorganize different aspects of the job to come up with a different finished product.

EXPLANATION

Adaptive workers, more so than their innovative comrades, can handle (and generally enjoy) jobs that require accuracy and precision. They are tolerant of repetitive work, make fewer errors than innovators in performing the same task, and deal better with details. Compared with innovators, adapters are rule-followers. They dislike surprises and prefer predictability. They try to do things better, while innovators try to do things differently. If given a choice, adapters usually opt to work in a company rather than on their own, believing that a company provides security.

Innovators, on the other hand, have a strong need for variety in their daily activities. They try to handle several projects at once and tend to be risk-takers who try new twists on old routines. They like to experiment, and they trust their own resources when confronted with novelty. Adapters and innovators will always be found anywhere people are involved in a cooperative effort.

In Kirton's book *Management Initiative*, he concludes that on a scale between adapter and innovator, most people fall in the middle. The adapter-innovator continuum is so prevalent, it even distinguishes work styles in the political arena. According to James David Barber, author of *The Presidential Character*, William Howard Taft, Warren Harding, and Dwight D. Eisenhower were essentially adaptive presidents, while Franklin D. Roosevelt, Harry S. Truman, and John F. Kennedy were primarily innovators.

Adapters and innovators often make excellent teammates, whether in work, friendship, or love. More often than not, they tend to balance each other out. It might be interesting to compare answers with your spouse, partner, or close friend to see if your traits are mutually complementary.

Will You Land the Job of Your Dreams?

In today's market, landing a job is more difficult than keeping one. Personnel managers see the interview as crucial. Droves of job seekers fall by the wayside because of a poor showing during the first five or ten minutes of the initial meeting. On the other hand, a successful interview generally leads to a job offer.

A study conducted at Columbia University in New York revealed that an average worker over thirty-five years of age changes jobs every three years. What's more, workers under thirty-five make the switch about every eighteen months. According to these statistics, you will probably be interviewed for a job within the next three years. Chances are you may develop a case of anticipatory anxiety about how you'll fare in the interview. Perhaps the following quiz will help.

TEST

Turn the tables for a moment. Pretend you are the interviewer. Assume that your company (TechAll) is an average firm and the job candidate is of average competence. The applicant has given the following responses to your questions—do they seem acceptable to you?

1. Q: Why are you leaving your present position?

A: I didn't get along with my boss; we had different temperaments.

Acceptable *Unacceptable*

2. Q: What do you know about TechAll?

A: It has 475 employees, is seventeen years old, profits are up 10 percent this year, and you've recently upgraded your product, which *Forbes* says is likely to be more in demand in the next decade.

Acceptable *Unacceptable*

3. Q: Why would you be an asset to this company?

A: Well, objectively speaking, I would say that I'm diligent, smart, and very willing to get the work done.

Acceptable *Unacceptable*

4. Q: Why have you had four jobs in the past seven years?

A: I wanted to better myself, so when better-paying jobs came up, I took them.

Acceptable *Unacceptable*

5. Q: You've had the same job for nine years—ever since college. Didn't you think this would limit your career prospects?

A: Things were going well. The company kept promoting me, offering more responsibility and more money, so I stayed there.

Acceptable *Unacceptable*

6. Q: Why should we hire you?

A: I'm known as a fast learner. In my past position, I reorganized and computerized the twelve-person department and was promoted to supervisor in eight months.

Acceptable *Unacceptable*

7. Q: Why did you leave your last job after only two months?

A: I didn't realize it would be so dull and repetitive. Also, there wasn't any place to move up in the firm.

Acceptable *Unacceptable*

8. Q: Why have you been unemployed for seven months?

A: The job market was poor, so I opted to take college courses toward my degree and work on a voluntary community project.

Acceptable *Unacceptable*

9. Q: Tell me about a project that didn't work out well and was a disappointment to you or your boss.

A: Well, I really can't think of anything of significance. All the projects I worked on went pretty well.

Acceptable *Unacceptable*

10. Q: Are there any questions you would like to ask me about the duties of the position?

A: Yes. What are the exact working hours, vacation periods, medical benefits, and pension plan?

Acceptable *Unacceptable*

SCORING

Read the explanation section to discover how well you were able to gauge the most appropriate responses to these types of interview questions. The average person gets about five questions correct.

EXPLANATION

1. *Unacceptable.* Personality clashes are never commendable, and there's no assurance that this will not be a problem at TechAll. A more acceptable answer would relate to differences in job approach or work philosophy between the applicant and his former boss.

2. *Acceptable.* Here you're getting solid evidence that the applicant has done his homework about TechAll. The applicant is prepared for the question.

3. *Unacceptable.* Self-praise is usually no recommendation. These claims are general and hard to prove. A better answer would be one that gives solid, verifiable facts, such as: "I procured good loan credit for ACME at four banks in the area, and two years ago I was given the Productive Employee of the Year award by our local Chamber of Commerce."

4. *Unacceptable.* The impetus for changing jobs was not career growth or acquisition of new skills, but money. Interviewers can be dismayed to hear that monetary gain is an applicant's only motivation.

5. *Acceptable.* True, the applicant stayed on the job for a long time, but he showed signs of career growth and advancement.

6. *Acceptable.* Interviewers here are fishing for a sign of self-confidence and a readiness to show it. Usually a succinct, generalized statement of provable skills and favorable work traits will suffice.

7. *Unacceptable.* The applicant was unrealistic to expect advancement in two months. Also, had the candidate done some research, he would have foreseen the weak possibilities for advancement and personal fulfillment before taking the job.

8. *Acceptable.* Time lapses between jobs happen to even the most qualified candidates. Interviewers like to hear that applicants used this time constructively.

9. *Unacceptable.* No one is perfect. Applicants who imply that their work performance was flawless are probably bending the truth. Be open but brief about admitting past mistakes.

10. *Unacceptable.* An applicant is judged by his questions as well as his answers. Here the applicant's inquiries reveal that he is more concerned with short-term personal gains than with how much of a contribution he can make to the company as a whole. An applicant's questions should show that he is interested in specific functions of the firm and how his skills would fit those functions. Granted, fringe benefits are important, but he can always find this out later.

Would You Be an Understanding Boss?

Job dissatisfaction is rampant these days, running as high as 70 percent in some industries. In a tight job market, the figure is probably even higher. Most of the time workers are disgruntled because they feel misunderstood by those in charge. Often, supervisors don't accurately read the signals of workers who are growing progressively discontent with their work. Furthermore, because many supervisors are job-oriented rather than people-oriented, they sometimes lack the skills to react appropriately when they do spot employee unrest.

Chances are that if you work for a company, you've thought of leaving it a few times in the past year. Or perhaps you've had a fantasy or two of how you could run the whole corporation better than your president does. So let's say that by some stroke of magic, you're suddenly placed in charge of your department or company. How well would you fare? Would you be perceptive enough to identify symptoms of worker unrest before they eroded into labor-management chaos? Your judgments as manager would be influenced by how you perceive your workers and what you believe is important to them.

TEST

Below is a ten-statement quiz that relates to happiness on the job. How understanding a boss would you be?

1. Men enjoy their jobs more than women do.
True *False*

2. If a worker is dissatisfied he will produce less.
True *False*

3. Job satisfaction tends to increase with age.
True *False*

4. Men tend to rely upon their supervisors for job satisfaction more than women do.
True *False*

5. New employees tend to show high job satisfaction.
True *False*

6. Increasing workers' salaries improves their level of job contentment most of the time.
True *False*

7. Compared with high performers, low performers will do better if you provide them more chances to socialize on the job.
True *False*

8. The more intelligent a worker, the more satisfied he or she tends to be.
True *False*

9. Job dissatisfaction tends to increase with a worker's level of responsibility.
True *False*

10. Hours and work conditions are generally not important factors in job satisfaction.
True *False*

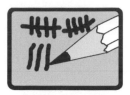

SCORING

This is a difficult quiz and you may be in for a few surprises. To tally your score, give yourself 1 point for each response that matches yours. All the statements were drawn from recent industry surveys.

1. *False*   **2.** *False*   **3.** *False*   **4.** *False*   **5.** *False*   **6.** *False*   **7.** *True*   **8.** *True*   **9.** *False*
10. *True*

A score of 5 is average. Anything above 5 indicates that you have a better-than-average understanding of what makes workers happy.

EXPLANATION

The major studies on job satisfaction in the U.S. go back to just after World War II. The Conference Board, a non-profit research organization formerly known as the National Labor Relations Board, did a significant and still much quoted study in 1947. Basically, it found that management had little idea about what workers considered the most satisfying aspects of their jobs.

For example, management put more emphasis on wages than workers did. On a list of the top ten most important aspects of the job, workers ranked salary third on the list, while managers assumed it was workers' number one aspect of job satisfaction. Workers actually ranked security the most important aspect of their jobs, while managers ranked it second on the list. Similarly, workers placed the possibility of advancement higher on their list than management did. The largest discrepancy between workers and management was in the importance placed on job benefits: workers ranked this their fourth most pressing concern, while management considered this only eighth in order of importance.

As if these disparities in work values weren't enough to cause friction between labor and management, a report by the Department of Health, Education and Welfare, called "Work in America," yielded other previously ignored factors found to cause job blahs. It stated that worker frustration is only partially due to poor management philosophy and work conditions. Worker alienation is also related to a variety of social problems such as physical and mental health, family stability, and community acceptance.

So, given all this, it's plain to see that the boss who tries to keep everyone happy must bear a lot in mind. Still think you'd like to be one?

Does Your Job Satisfy Your Personality Needs?

Lifelong satisfaction in a job is rare. Some 70 percent of all workers are dissatisfied with what they do and would welcome a change. For the remaining relatively content 30 percent, there's a significant reason why we continue in our jobs. The fact is we enjoy work that fulfills our deeper needs and thinking styles. Unfortunately, most of us don't probe our psychodynamics before we choose a job. We all might be better off if we did.

While a professor of management at the University of Southern California, Dr. Alan Rowe uncovered several crucial factors that relate to happy work adjustment. He identified four basic thinking styles. When we match these styles with what our job requires, the chances are good we'll be professionally satisfied.

If you feel unhappy with your position and wonder if a change will help you live up to more of your potential, the quiz below might help. It is based on a test devised by Rowe after some six years of research, and it will suggest whether you and your job are meant for each other.

TEST

For each of the ten items below, choose two answers from among the lettered choices. Put the number 2 next to your first letter choice for each item, and the number 1 next to your second letter choice. (It may help to make a table with the letters a, b, c, and d across the top and the question numbers 1 through 10 along the left-hand side; then, for each question, simply place the 2 and 1 beneath the letter choices you've picked.)

1. I enjoy jobs that:
2 *a.* Have much variety   *b.* Involve people *c.* Allow independent action   *d.* Are technical and defined

2. My main objective is to:
a. Be the best in my field *b.* Feel secure in my job.
2 *c.* Get recognition for my work   *d.* Have a status position

3. When faced with a problem, I:
a. Apply careful analysis *b.* Rely on my feelings
2 *c.* Look for creative paths   *d.* Rely on proven approaches

4. When uncertain about what to do, I:
a. Search for facts   *b.* Delay making a decision
2 *c.* Explore a possible compromise *d.* Rely on hunches and intuition

5. Whenever possible, I avoid:
2 *a.* Incomplete work   *b.* Conflict with others
1 *c.* Using numbers or formulas   *d.* Long debates

6. In social settings I generally:
a. Think about what is being said   *b.* Listen to conversations *c.* Observe what is going on 2 *d.* Speak with others

7. I am good at remembering:

a. Places where I met people [1] **b.** People's personalities [2] **c.** People's faces **d.** People's names

8. Others consider me:

a. Disciplined and precise **b.** Supportive and compassionate [1] **c.** Imaginative and perfectionist [2] **d.** Aggressive and domineering

9. I dislike:

a. Boring work [1] **b.** Being rejected **c.** Following rules **d.** Losing control of others

10. I am especially good at:

a. Solving difficult problems [1] **b.** Interacting with others [2] **c.** Seeing many possibilities **d.** Recalling dates and facts

---

SCORING

A	B	C	D
7	4	14	5

(30)

Tally up the number values you've assigned to each letter. The two letters that have the highest scores correspond to your two major thinking styles, as defined in the "Explanation" section that follows.

EXPLANATION

A. Analytical. *(2nd)* Analytical people are problem solvers. They have a desire to find the best possible answers. They examine lots of details and use large amounts of data. They are innovative, creative, and enjoy variety.

B. Behavioral. Behavioral people need human contacts. They are supportive, empathic people. They use little data in making decisions, preferring to talk things out with others. They communicate easily and prefer to use persuasion instead of pressure to win their point of view.

 C. Conceptual. *(1st)* Conceptual people are broad-minded thinkers who like to contemplate the "big picture." They are future-oriented and achievement-oriented and tend to be independent, humanistic, and creative.

D. Directive. Directive people are authoritarian taskmasters. They need power and expect results. They act decisively and are rule- and regulation-minded. They are highly verbal and tend to rely on intuition.

These patterns predict the kind of work that might suit a person best. Businesspeople, for example, tend to score high on the analytical and conceptual scales. They like to consider many options and develop broad plans for their companies. Technical people, engineers, scientists, and others in similar lines of work are analytical and directive. They enjoy solving problems logically, working with numbers, and finding mathematical and scientific answers.

Those in the helping arts, like nurses, doctors, and social workers, combine conceptual and behavioral frames of mind. They like to work closely with people in developing an understanding of human affairs. People who combine the analytical-behavioral frameworks tend to go into the fields of education and law, while directive-behavioral people are often found in sales and politics.

The highest score obtainable in any category is 50, but few people ever make this. The closer your score is to 50, the stronger your thinking style is in that category. Match your thinking style with your current job, and consider how well your work satisfies your personality needs.

What's Your Pecuniary Profile?

Money. Throughout history, wars have been fought over it, religions have denounced it as a danger to one's soul, and most crimes have been committed for it, in one way or another. Money is a powerful motivator. When it beckons, many people have difficulty resisting its call.

No matter what our economic level, we all have a "dollar personality," a cluster of attitudes about money. There are three basic "money personalities"—perhaps you'll see yourself in one of them.

Compulsive spenders: This group feels uneasy about holding on to money. They believe that if they accumulate earnings, then they must also bear the unwelcome responsibility for its management. This generates anxiety. Compulsive spenders feel emotionally secure when they're free to spend. Through buying and owning items, they gain a false sense of assurance and security.

Compulsive hoarders: Hoarders perceive money as an extension of their egos, and to them, giving up money is like losing a part of themselves. They have a compelling drive to keep and protect their cash as if it were their very lifeblood.

Compulsive risk-takers: These people are basically magical thinkers guided by a grandiose notion that they can win the universe if they wish hard enough for it. For them, winning at a game, gambling, or engaging in speculative business or stock ventures symbolizes immortality.

TEST

What is your dollar personality? The following quiz items measure specific attitudes you might possess but of which you are perhaps unaware.

1. To be rich means to be powerful.
True *False*

2. The bottom line is, money is the ultimate symbol of success.
True *False*

3. I like to buy top-of-the-line products.
True *False*

4. I often use money to persuade others to do what I want.
True *False*

5. When I discover that I earn more than someone I previously believed made more than I, I feel satisfied.
True *False*

6. I'm likely to tell people how much I paid for an expensive item, even if they don't ask.
True *False*

7. I have been told or have later realized that I boasted about how much money I earn.
True *False*

8. I feel flattered when people notice a prestigious label on something I own.
True *False*

9. I try to find out who makes more money than I do.
True *False*

10. I catch myself admiring those who have more money than I have.
True *False*

11. When I shop, I am frequently mindful of what others will think about the quality of my purchases.
True *False*

12. I really enjoy it when I'm complimented on my expensive possessions.
True *False*

SCORING

To tally your score, give yourself 1 point for each "True" response. Read on for an explanation of your spending style.

A score of 10–12 points: You believe that money equals power and prestige, which mean a lot to you. External recognition and regard by others are vital to your feelings of importance and success. You might look down on those whom you think are worth less than you or decline to consider them for friendship. You might want to soften your attitudes.

A score of 6–9 points: You are average in your tendency to use money for social power and status. You probably try to satisfy those needs through other channels, such as personal achievement and relationships.

A score of 0–5 points: No matter how much money you have, you don't use money to enhance your image with others. You evaluate yourself and others by their intangible qualities, not by their possessions. If you do pursue money, it is for reasons other than the need for social power and prestige.

EXPLANATION

The quiz above is based on research conducted by K. T. Yamauchi and D. I. Templer at the California School of Professional Psychology in Fresno. In an effort to develop a scale for measuring attitudes towards money, Yamauchi and Templer tested three hundred people at various economic levels. The quiz taps into the tendency to regard money as a means to social power, prestige, and status.

In an interesting aside, attitudes about money are an important predictor of marital compatibility. If you're married, or plan to be, and you and your partner have very different "money personalities," there may be trouble ahead. It has been noted that couples argue most often about money, and it is the number one cause of divorce. These rifts usually have more to do with who has the power to make important decisions than about the money itself. It might be wise for couples to compare their attitudes towards money before they get married in order to pinpoint potential areas of disagreement.

Are You Ready for a Job Switch?

When Sharon started her job as an editorial assistant at a newspaper four years ago, she was eager to succeed. Now she shows all the telltale signs of the job blahs. She lapses into long fantasies about traveling, socializes a lot, and has been speaking more and more with friends about their fields of work.

According to the research, job unhappiness is the rule rather than the exception. Not surprisingly, the lower someone is on the company ladder, the more discontent he or she feels. It has been estimated that 50 percent of the work force, like Sharon, are also unhappy with their jobs. And often these toilers won't even admit it to themselves.

TEST

Are you ready for a job change? To find out, take the following quiz.

1. Within the past six months, I have made more errors at work than usual.
True   False

2. I am rarely sick on my days off, but have many stress-related illnesses at work.
True   False

3. I can't imagine any job-related surprises.
True   False

4. I acquired at least five new skills in the past year to make my job easier.
True   False

5. I talk very little about my job when with friends.
True   False

6. Most of the time, I am uncomfortable mixing socially with people in my line of work.
True   False

7. I am probably paid too little for what I do, but I enjoy the job security.
True   False

8. I am generally cynical about my vocation when approached by newcomers.
True   False

9. I read little or nothing about new developments and procedures in my field.
True   False

10. I seldom get new ideas for improving my job.
True   False

SCORING

To tally your score, give yourself 1 point for each "True" response, except for item 4—give yourself 1 point if you answered "False" on item 4.

A score of 0–4 points: Your job matches your skills and interests well, and you most likely receive satisfaction from it. You have a good chance of career success.

A score of 5–7 points: Your job compatibility is average. However, there's probably room for improvement. Are you doing all you can to develop new skills to move up the ranks?

A score of 8 points or more: You and your work are probably not well suited to each other. It's likely that you're ready for a job switch. Have you thought carefully about your career needs? A talk with a career advisor may be in order.

EXPLANATION

When Pope John XXIII was asked how many people worked at the Vatican, the witty pontiff quipped, "About half." Surely, if sophisticated surveys were done in even so reverent a place as the Holy City, they would have found a fair share of slackers who don't labor hard enough because of work dissatisfaction.

So, if your work output is down, you're unenthusiastic and careless in your work, and can do your job in your sleep (and sometimes do), it's likely you have the job blahs. Poor judgment in selecting a job is often the reason for work woes later on. David Wheeler and Irving Janis, authors of *A Practical Guide for Making Decisions*, conclude that most people move from job to job haphazardly. Often they accept new posts for the money and fail to carefully weigh the pros and cons of the job or think about its relevance to their ultimate goal of career advancement.

Moreover, studies at Yale University confirm that being miscast in a job can cause stress and maladjustment, which can lead to family disruptions. A person may resent having to work, or may feel indignant about working above or below his or her level of competence. These frustrations can easily be transferred to one's home life. The discontentment can also flow the other way, with an unhappy home life leading to problems at work. So, it's wise to also explore all the other aspects of your life when you feel uneasy, restless, or bored with your job. On the bright side, once you do find a job more suited to you, studies have found that happy workers are more productive, and usually live longer, too.

Are You Slotted for Job Success?

A re you dissatisfied with your career? Do you wish you could do better? If so, do you sometimes wonder what's holding you back?

Career pros consistently find that job success is strongly related to a particular cluster of attitudes, habits, and personality traits. If you already have an impressive work history, you possess something a prospective employer wants. But if you're still in the process of building a solid background, you would benefit from knowing as much as possible about the traits that prospective employers value and reward.

TEST

The following quiz will gauge your grasp of what it takes to be a success on the job.

3 **1.** I get to work on time.
  a. *Rarely*   **b.** *Sometimes*   **c.** *Often*

3 **2.** I try hard to give a full day's work each day.
  a. *Rarely*   **b.** *Sometimes*   **c.** *Often*

2 **3.** I plan an alternate means of getting to work in case there's a transportation breakdown.
  a. *Rarely*   **b.** *Sometimes*   **c.** *Often*

2 **4.** I feel tired and sometimes even ill at work and yearn to have a good nap.
  a. *Rarely*   **b.** *Sometimes*   **c.** *Often*

3 **5.** I get along well with my co-workers and my boss.
  a. *Rarely*   **b.** *Sometimes*   **c.** *Often*

3 **6.** I accept supervision and rules without resistance or opposition, unless the situation calls for debate.
  a. *Rarely*   **b.** *Sometimes*   **c.** *Often*

3 **7.** I have enough education, training, and job know-how for the position I now hold.
  a. *Rarely*   **b.** *Sometimes*   **c.** *Often*

1 **8.** I have loyalty and respect for my company and its products.
  a. *Rarely*   **b.** *Sometimes*   **c.** *Often*

2 **9.** My grooming and appearance are always appropriate and attractive.
  a. *Rarely*   **b.** *Sometimes*   **c.** *Often*

3 **10.** My behavior is ethical, unpretentious, and courteous.
  a. *Rarely*   **b.** *Sometimes*   **c.** *Often*

SCORING

To tally your score, give yourself 1 point for each "a" response, 2 points for each "b" response, and 3 points for each "c" response.

A score of 24–30 points: You possess the attitudes and traits that make employers want to hire you.

A score of 17–23 points: A score in this range shows that you have an average number of job success traits. You should do as well as most of your peers.

A score of 10–16 points: You lack many of the job success traits necessary for a career upgrade, and it's probably apparent to your employer. You might benefit from reading a book or two about how to move up the corporate ladder. You might also want to go over your answers with a friend who can help you find your weak spots.

EXPLANATION

This quiz consists of the ten basic job success traits found to be most important in the minds of bosses. They were compiled by the U.S. Department of Labor from a survey of thousands of employers conducted in 2000. Read on for an expanded explanation of each item.

1. Surprisingly, many work hours are wasted by those who believe it is okay to be several minutes late. Employers are especially unhappy about the example such workers set for those who get to work on time or arrive early.

2. Nearly all businessmen in the survey spoke out emphatically about expecting a full day's work for a full day's pay. Some employees settle for just trying to look busy when someone is watching.

3. Successful workers plan ahead for those emergency situations when a car breaks down or the bus is late, and get to work on time despite obstacles.

4. Companies lose millions each month due to employee illness. Thus, a poor attendance record can ruin your chances for promotion. It's a sensitive issue among employers. Consequently, more firms offer "wellness" programs to promote mental and physical fitness. Incidentally, the data show that these programs improve production significantly.

5. A large percentage of those not promoted or fired fail because they lack the social skills needed to get along with co-workers or supervisors. Work flows better from person to person when people are compatible.

6. Unfortunately, many workers who hit a snag have not resolved their early conflicts with authority. At heart they are still restless adolescents who buck the system and resist following rules. Mature adults, on the other hand, show flexibility and do not feel diminished when accommodating the demands of their bosses.

7. The most common requirements for most jobs are education and training. Are you one of the millions who succeed by getting the schooling needed to qualify for better positions? (For example, by taking computer, business, or secretarial courses?)

8. If you honestly cannot feel in favor of your company and its products or services, it will be tough to make a wholehearted job commitment. Think twice before signing on with a firm where your loyalty will be difficult to give.

9. The kind of appearance that is valued by employers varies from job to job. Receptionists, for example, must be well dressed, groomed, and attractive, while file clerks and others who work in the "background" of a company can usually adapt more casual dress codes. But no matter what the job, appearance is a powerful factor that influences your supervisor's evaluation of you.

10. Companies spend millions using lie detectors, reference checks, and personal interviews in screening applicants. In this day and age of computer banks loaded with information on work histories, it does not pay to be anything but honest and ethical on your job or when presenting your work history to a prospective boss.

Could You Be Your Own Boss?

How often have you attended a meeting only to hear a new idea mentioned and lament, "I thought of that months ago"? The fact is that many employees have ideas on how to streamline company operations, or about new marketing strategies. But too often those ideas are not voiced because of a fear of rejection, or because of a high regard for the status quo.

If you are holding back your thoughts, you may be doing yourself and your company a disservice. Having a hand in how well the company does can increase your satisfaction with your job. It can also boost company profits—and that makes management happy.

In fact, many successful innovations have been introduced this way. Gifford Pinchot III, a management consultant in New Haven, Connecticut, coined the term "intrapreneur" to describe those responsible for such innovations. In his book, *Intrapreneuring*, Pinchot defines such a person as "the dreamer who introduces new or improved products, processes, and services in his or her company of employment."

TEST

Could you be an intrapreneur? The following quiz may reveal the answer. Even if you don't have a paying job outside the home, consider what you do most (attend school, do volunteer work, etc.) and answer the questions as they relate to that activity. The same general principles apply.

1. You spend a lot of time thinking about ways to make aspects of your job run more smoothly, in terms of refining or perfecting techniques, methods, and equipment.

True   False

2. You receive positive feedback at work when you suggest changes.

True   False

3. You are persistent in pushing ahead with a project, even when it looks as if you might fail.

True   False

4. You get excited about your work when thinking or talking about it.

True   False

5. You frequently come up with better ways of doing things at home, at play, and in the community.

True   False

6. You can visualize the concrete steps you need to take in order to turn your ideas into action.

True   False

7. You are willing to give up some of your free time and/or salary in order to try out new ideas if success means reward somewhere down the line.

True   False

8. You often compare the way your boss does things to the way you'd do them if you were in charge.

True   False

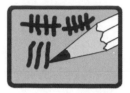

SCORING

If you answered "True" to five or more quiz items, you show definite signs of being an intrapreneur.

EXPLANATION

The quiz items are adapted from Pinchot's book, and identify an entrepreneurial type of personality. When you have this type of personality and it is manifested under the umbrella of a company setting, you can be considered an intrapreneur. A blend of the independent entrepreneur and the company man or woman may seem unlikely, yet this is precisely what Pinchot says can be done, and he cites many successful examples of such an amalgam.

One such intrapraneur is Chuck House of the computer firm Hewlett-Packard. House didn't leave the fold, yet he achieved outstanding success as an inventor of a special video-display tube. It was used on the first U.S. lunar landing and in the first heart transplant ever performed. House achieved his goal by privately researching the tube's potential, estimating its marketability, then persuading management to produce and sell it.

In short, the intrapreneur works around office protocol to seek out ways of fulfilling his need for personal achievement. Intrapreneuring, of course, has been around for generations in one form or another, as companies gave their more productive workers leeway to pursue new ideas. But Pinchot asserts that it's time for this movement to get fully underway. As a consultant on intrapraneuring for major corporations like Exxon, Ford, and AT&T, he argues: "If big companies want to quicken the pace of innovation, they must honor and empower intrapreneurs."

If you tested well on the quiz and aren't already working on your own, you may want to test your intrapreneurial abilities in your work setting. If you succeed, you may consider striking out on your own one day.

Are You a Workaholic?

Work is their only way of life. Their philosophy is, "Better to wear out than to rust out." They catch late night trains, rarely take vacations, and incidentally, usually rise to the top of the corporate ladder. Who are they? They are workaholics—those tireless toilers of our society.

Dr. Marilyn Machlowitz, author of *Workaholics*, estimates that about 5 percent of all American adults are workaholics. They exist on all levels: butchers, farmers, housewives, and executives. But no matter what their occupation, they all share common characteristics, marked by a similar set of personality traits.

R15/ kpedk

TEST

If you've ever thought that you work too hard, you just may be a workaholic. Compare your score on this quiz to that on "Do You Suffer from Sunday Neurosis," page 123.

1. You do more than two hours of important office work daily at home or while commuting.
True *False*

2. You often eat lunch while working.
True *False*

3. You are time-conscious no matter what you're doing.
True *False*

4. It is important for you to win at everything, including family games.
True *False*

5. Compared with your peers, you set higher goals for yourself.
True *False*

6. You often suggest to your boss ways to make your job more productive.
True *False*

7. You grow restless when there is little to do except relax.
True *False*

8. You tend to skip social events because of work duties.
True *False*

9. Compared with most people, you have few close friends.
True *False*

10. You feel vaguely uneasy after a day of doing absolutely nothing constructive.
True *False*

11. When an interesting work project arises, you find it hard to resist.
True *False*

12. When sick, you reluctantly stay home, feeling that no one is competent enough to handle your job.
True *False*

SCORING

Workaholics answer "True" to every question in this quiz. To tally your score, give yourself 1 point for each "True" response, then read the categories below to determine how much of a workaholic you are.

A score of 1–4 points: Your achievement drive is low. There are things in life other than work that you find satisfying. You don't welcome added job responsibilities, and tense up when challenges come your way. Work that is predictable and clear-cut is best for you.

A score of 5–8 points: You are adept at balancing work with other non-work related activities. You try to get ahead at work but draw the line when your job intrudes on your personal life. Periods of busyness mixed with relaxation are what you prefer at work.

A score of 9–12 points: You are a classic workaholic. You suffer from a manmade affliction that has its rewards and its punishments. In your mind, to slow down means to fail. You enjoy being on the go, but you vaguely sense that there is a compulsive quality to your way of life.

EXPLANATION

Dr. Machlowitz, who interviewed more than 100 workaholics, has both good and bad news to report. Workaholics inflict suffering on others who have to adjust to their frenetic pace. They demand, push, and compete their way to the top of their companies. However, she notes, workaholics are amazingly happy, and are among the most productive people in our society. Though weighed down by work, they are the restless doers who accomplish audacious yet constructive projects that benefit us all. To understand yourself or another workaholic better, read the following section, which explains in greater detail the reasons the typical workaholic would answer "True" to each question on the quiz.

Items 1, 2, and 3: Workaholics hate to waste time, and they often do two or more things at once. They are very time-conscious, and schedule daily activities in accordance with how long it takes to complete given tasks. They are often late for appointments because they can't bear to squander time waiting for the other person to arrive. Often they work right up to a deadline to complete a task.

Item 4: More often than not, workaholics are competitive. They strive to excel when pitted against others. But, it must also be said, they compete most vigorously with none other than themselves.

Item 5: Strivers tend to set high goals for themselves. Most people set a level of achievement for themselves that is slightly above their actual performance capability, but the workaholic aims significantly higher than his or her performance level. When there is a disparity between what he or she aspires to achieve and what he or she actually accomplishes, the workaholic is much more frustrated than the average person.

Items 6 and 7: Work addicts grow restless when they don't have work to do. Often they create their own challenges by adding new duties to their jobs. Hence, they have a compulsion to take on more and more assignments through which they can reaffirm their competence.

Items 8 and 9: Because of their all-consuming preoccupation with work, workaholics often have little interest in socializing. According to Dr. Machlowitz, they are unable to maintain intimate relationships, and instead, develop a closeness with their work.

Items 10 and 11: Dr. John Neulinger, author of *The Psychology of Leisure*, declares that many workaholics suffer from leisure phobia—a fear of having nothing constructive to do with their free time. Viennese psychoanalyst Sandor Ferenczi has called this "weekend" or "Sunday" neurosis. (See the following quiz to test whether you have this).

Item 12: Psychologist Wayne E. Oates of the University of Louisville, Kentucky, who has written widely on the subject, believes workaholics build their own egos by creating an image of being irre-placeable. They have difficulty delegating work to others because they feel the job can't be done as well as they could do it.

Do You Suffer from Sunday Neurosis?

It's a Sunday morning, and you have a free day ahead of you. But you're already worrying about how you'll fill it up—will you do errands, tinker around the house, make plans with friends? For many of us who work full-time, figuring out how to spend our free time becomes a job in itself. We eagerly await the arrival of the weekend, but when it finally comes, we feel threatened by the idea of being leisurely.

Many of us long for free time, but then fail to truly enjoy it. Why? Because we're living in the imperative mood! We've been swallowed up by the quick tempo of our society. We must be doing something, anything, just to fill up empty time and relieve some indefinable sense of guilt. It's what psychoanalyst Karen Horney has called "the tyranny of the should": I should be doing this or I should be doing that—but above all, I shouldn't waste time.

This behavior has been called the "Sunday Neurosis." It attacks on weekends and vacations, when we're faced with time on our hands. It makes us restless and almost panicky. But when Monday morning rolls around, we once again feel pacified.

TEST

Do some of these behaviors seem to describe you? If so, the following quiz may indicate whether your difficulty in managing your free time means you that you have "leisure phobia."

1. It bothers me to waste time.
True *False*

2. I get more fun out of my job than I do from my free-time activities.
True *False*

3. I am an impatient person.
True *False*

4. I really don't need as much playtime as the average person seems to need.
True *False*

5. I enjoy working and playing rapidly.
True *False*

6. I usually get bored sooner than most others on a long train or plane trip.
True *False*

7. When I play, I try harder to win than the average person.
True *False*

8. I usually thrive on activities that keep me on the go and require my full attention.
True *False*

9. I consider myself an assertive person.
True *False*

10. I usually have difficulty finding satisfying things to do in my spare time.
True *False*

SCORING

Give yourself 1 point for each "True" response.

A score of 7 points or less: You are free enough of anxiety to enjoy your leisure time.

A score of 8 points or more: You have a tendency toward the common malady of our time, "hurry sickness." You probably struggle to enjoy your free time.

EXPLANATION

This quiz is based on the clinical analysis of people who become frustrated with unstructured time on their hands. Researchers have determined that there are some helpful tools we can employ to overcome this fear of freedom.

First, be sure your leisure time is not too crowded with things to do. Leave plenty of time between activities and try to keep pressure off. If you have something planned for the afternoon, relax and enjoy a late breakfast or brunch. Try to see this not as wasting time but as giving yourself a chance to let go and unwind. Try to engage in an activity that you don't normally have time for, like going on a long bike ride, or making a big dinner that requires lots of preparation. You'll feel good about your accomplishments, and you'll also satisfy your internal requirements for being productive.

And bear in mind some ancient wisdom. An old Chinese proverb says: "To be for one day entirely at leisure is to be for one day an immortal." Will you have your day of immortality?

Are You Burned Out?

Burnout is a modern affliction. It affects all types of people, especially those who work under pressure, deal frequently with others, and expect a lot from themselves. It is particularly prevalent among those who tend to set unrealistic goals for themselves, a by-product of having an unflappable drive to succeed and an excess of external pressure. Often such people grow bored with and unresponsive to their work, taking too long to make even the simplest decisions, and completing the most basic tasks in twice the usual time. For burnout victims, life is not as fulfilling as it might be.

Some critics say that the burnout syndrome is nothing new, that it is simply depression with a new label. But there is evidence that burnout differentiates itself from depression, and that both its cause and remedy are distinctive.

Psychologist Herbert Freudenberger discusses the unique qualities of this modern-day malady in his book *Burn-Out: The High Cost of High Achievement*. In it, he describes how burnout occurs in students, workers, and family members, and offers sound solutions to combat it.

TEST

To find out if you are fighting with the frazzles, take the following quiz, which is adapted from Freudenberger's book. Rate yourself in terms of the five-point scale that follows each question, where 1 equals "a little bit" and 5 equals "very much so."

1. Do you seem to be working harder and accomplishing less?
A little bit **1 2 3 4 (5)** *Very much so*

2. Do you tire more easily?
A little bit **1 2 3 4 (5)** *Very much so*

3. Do you often get the blues for no apparent reason?
A little bit **1 2 3 4 (5)** *Very much so*

4. Do you forget appointments, deadlines, and/or personal possessions?
A little bit **1 (2) 3 4 5** *Very much so*

5. Have you become increasingly irritable?
A little bit **1 2 3 4 (5)** *Very much so*

6. Have you grown more disappointed in those around you?
A little bit **1 2 3 (4) 5** *Very much so*

7. Do you see close friends and family members less frequently than you used to?
A little bit **1 2 (3) 4 5** *Very much so*

8. Do you suffer physical symptoms like pains and headaches?
A little bit **1 2 3 4 (5)** *Very much so*

9. Do you find it hard to laugh when the joke is on you?
A little bit **1 2 (3) 4 5** *Very much so*

10. Does sex seem more trouble than it's worth?
A little bit **(1) 2 3 4 5** *Very much so*

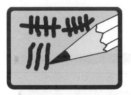

SCORING

Where do you stand on the Burnout Scale? To tally your score, add the total number of points from each response.

A score of 0–15 points: You may be stressed out on occasion, but generally you're doing fine.

A score of 16–24 points: You're a candidate for burnout. You may want to take a step back and assess how to relax a bit.

A score of 25–29 points: You're beginning to burn out and should think about changing your work environment or lifestyle to give yourself more breathing room.

A score of 30 points or more: Cool it! You're suffering from burnout. Take whatever steps are necessary to alleviate some stress—you're in a dangerous situation that may pose a threat to your physical and mental well-being.

EXPLANATION

It has been said that next to the job of air-traffic controller, the occupation of police officer is the most stressful. Dr. William Kroes, former head of stress research at the National Institute of Occupational Safety (NIOS), concluded that there is more burnout among police officers than any other profession or occupation.

But burnout isn't only connected to a job. It can occur in anyone in a state of fatigue or frustration brought about by a devotion to a cause, a way of life, or a relationship that has failed to produce expected rewards. There are times when we all experience some minor burnout, when we are less than enthusiastic about shouldering our continual job responsibilities, but in time we usually snap out of it and once again take on our tasks.

If your score is high or if you have frequent periods of minor burnout, don't ignore the warning signs. This stressful state is reversible no matter how severe it is. Sometimes all that is needed to re-motivate you is a breather from the constant pressure or monotony of your life patterns. This can mean taking a vacation, getting a new job assignment, meeting new people, or getting a new perspective on your goals. Try to learn exactly what it is you have done in the past that seemed to revitalize you, then concentrate on doing it more often.

CHAPTER 6

The Smell of Success

"How are things otherwise?"

Are You Living Up to Your Super Potential?

Some years ago, a family friend who was pregnant visited us. She related that her baby was two weeks overdue. Attempting to understand our friend's dismay, my five-year-old son David tried to console her by saying, "Don't feel so bad, Mrs. Hays. After all, nobody's perfect."

Indeed, no one is perfect, and no one knows this better than human relations professionals. Psychologists have expounded on the theme of man's development, using terms like "self-actualization," "becoming," and "human fulfillment" to describe the human growth process at all levels—physical, psychological, and spiritual.

No matter how humble or exalted, we all move toward realizing our basic potential. This is evidenced in a child who studies to pass a test, a businessperson who does volunteer work in the community, or an athlete who tries to break a record. It is a continuing process of fulfilling our capacities.

The late Dr. Abraham Maslow pointed out that our inner nature, though it may be abused or misunderstood, "persists underground and [is] forever pressing for actualization." In other words, in the process of attaining our goals, we strive to fulfill our potential.

Behavioral scientists have identified indicators that reveal whether or not we are fulfilling our potential. For fifteen years, behavioral scientist Ronald Taft conducted a series of studies to identify those people who power their potential. He calls them "ego permissive" types. The following quiz is adapted from Taft's questionnaires.

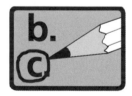

TEST

To what degree are you a self-actualizer? Your answers will require some fairly intense introspection.

1. I enjoy trying to see shapes in the clouds.
a. Not true   *b. Somewhat true*   *c. Very true*

2. More so than the average person, I believe I have had experiences that were both strange and wonderful.
a. Not true   *b. Somewhat true*   *c. Very true*

3. I like dressing up for Halloween or costume parties.
a. Not true   *b. Somewhat true*   *c. Very true*

4. I have had the feeling of being completely serene and at peace with the world.
a. Not true   *b. Somewhat true*   *c. Very true*

5. I can comprehend the depth of devotion a person may have that would make him willing to sacrifice his own life for someone he loves.
a. Not true   *b. Somewhat true*   *c. Very true*

6. I have been so involved with the characters in an absorbing book that I forgot my surroundings and lived the story with them.
a. Not true   *b. Somewhat true*   *c. Very true*

7. I have had profound fulfillment and satisfaction in creating a solution for something (as in crossword puzzles, craft projects, intellectual investigations, or a mystery story).

a. Not true *b. Somewhat true* *c. Very true*

8. I have had a "religious" experience that proved to me that a supernatural being exists.

a. Not true *b. Somewhat true* *c. Very true*

9. I have been so in love with someone that I was unconcerned about myself and extremely preoccupied with my beloved.

a. Not true *b. Somewhat true* *c. Very true*

10. I have had the experience of seeming to watch myself from a distance as if in a dream.

a. Not true *b. Somewhat true* *c. Very true*

SCORING

To tally your score, give yourself 1 point for each "a" response, 2 points for each "b" response, and 3 points for each "c" response.

A score of 15–20 points: You are in the average range of self-fulfillment.

A score of 21–27: It is likely that you are a self-actualizer. Keep striving to realize your goals and you should find greater contentment.

A score of 28–30: You are indeed a self-actualizer. But keep in mind that nobody's perfect—you, too, can keep striving for further contentment.

EXPLANATION

The items on the quiz may not appear to relate to what you might think of as indicating "self-actualization." The term might have brought to mind thoughts of achieving lofty, heroic goals. But there's sound reasoning behind the quiz items.

Dr. Maslow, whose personality theories are world famous, described self-actualized people as those who, from time to time, have "peak experiences," like those described in the quiz. These are moments when an individual has supremely intense and pleasurable feelings of a keen awareness of life. Maslow saw these as almost mystical experiences, in which a person loses or goes beyond his ordinary sense of self. At that moment, one is "at the peak" of his or her powers, using all of his or her capabilities to the fullest. Presumably, the more one has such experiences, the more he or she is a self-actualizer.

Being a self-actualizer is not dependent on your social status or occupation. Some other important signs of living to the fullest are accepting yourself for what you are and other people for what they are; being spontaneous; being concerned with ethical human values; and feeling that you have some mission or reason for your life.

Does Crisis Paralyze or Propel You?

All of us face crisis and stress, yet we differ in our capacity to cope with it. Some may seek professional counsel, while others may choose to deal with it on their own. No matter how we decide to face it, confronting crisis usually makes us stronger.

How we handle stress depends largely on our perception of it, which is influenced early on by our parents. At one extreme, some people see adversity as a dire event that renders one helpless and dooms one to suffering. At the other extreme, it can be perceived as a momentary barrier that can be overcome through strength and composure.

TEST

Where do you stand on the crisis-confrontation issue? How are you managing life's stresses? Take the following quiz to find out.

1. I am pessimistic about things that usually turn out okay in the long run.
a. Seldom   *b.* Sometimes   *c.* Often

2. My anger or irritation is out of proportion to what certain situations, such as traffic delays or slow service at a restaurant, warrant.
a. Seldom   *b.* Sometimes   *c.* Often

3. I need a drink or tranquilizer before facing a tough situation.
a. Seldom   *b.* Sometimes   *c.* Often

4. If I must make a quick decision, I don't take action until it is too late.
a. Seldom   *b.* Sometimes   *c.* Often

5. When the pressure is on, I am bothered by physical symptoms such as headaches, stomach cramps, lower back pain, and fatigue.
a. Seldom   *b.* Sometimes   *c.* Often

6. When something is bugging me, I am reluctant to meet new friends or go out socially.
a. Seldom   *b.* Sometimes   *c.* Often

7. When I worry, my sleep is restless and I have bad dreams.
a. Seldom   *b.* Sometimes   *c.* Often

8. If I'm worried, I can't seem to concentrate when I read.
a. Seldom   *b.* Sometimes   *c.* Often

9. When stress hits, I can't find satisfaction in the things I do.
a. Seldom   *b.* Sometimes   *c.* Often

10. If I'm under pressure, my habits change. For example, I sleep too much or too little, I overeat or don't eat enough, or I smoke or drink excessively.
a. Seldom   *b.* Sometimes   *c.* Often

SCORING

To tally your score, give yourself 1 point for each "a" response, 2 points for each "b" response, and 3 points for each "c."

A score of 10–16 points: You are coping well with most day-to-day urgencies, and overall enjoy emotional well-being.

A score of 17–24 points: You are handling your stress in an average and acceptable manner, which probably means that you are happy most of the time.

A score of 25–30 points: You tend to get bogged down by the tensions of daily living. Perhaps you are going through a temporary strain. Ask yourself: "Am I consistently less efficient in my daily routines?" If so, you may need to modify your reactions to stress.

EXPLANATION

Any upset, such as job stress or a physical illness, may trigger a temporary swing away from your normal living patterns. Though the behaviors listed in this quiz are universal, the difference between adequate and poor stress management depends on three factors: the intensity of the symptoms, how long they last, and how much they impair your functioning.

If someone with decent stress-management skills loses his or her job, he or she might show anxiety for a few weeks and have difficulty focusing on simple, everyday tasks, such as balancing a checkbook. For most people, these symptoms will fade as soon as they resume normal life patterns. But someone with a reduced capacity for handling heavy stress may show longer-lasting signs of maladjustment. If you feel that you are consistently less efficient in your daily routines, you may be suffering from undue stress. Five telltale signs indicate a decreased capacity to cope well with crisis: (1) overreaction to situations and people; (2) significant health changes; (3) changes in natural functions; (4) social anxiety; and (5) an overall decline in life satisfaction. If these changes describe you, it might be wise to talk out your situation with an objective person who may be able to help. You may learn that the root of the problem is not stress itself, but rather the manner in which you cope with life's ups and downs.

Are You Too Rigid?

If you ever watched the TV series *The Odd Couple*, you surely noticed a sharp contrast between the two lead characters. Oscar is the laid-back, flexible type, while Felix is just the opposite—proper, exacting, and highly organized. For entertainment purposes, they were cast as extremes. If you watched several episodes, you'd have noticed that the rigid one always seemed to suffer the most when things went wrong.

In real life, rigidity poses the same problems. People who tend to be overly conscientious perfectionists can be hard on those who can't keep up with their demands, and as a result, tough on themselves, too. Most of us are neither extremely exacting nor extremely easygoing. Instead, we are usually a mix of both. Still, just as people are classified as introverts or extraverts, submissive or dominant, people can also be categorized as rigid or flexible. When people are uptight, however, stress is often a factor. Fortunately, we can learn to spot this tendency and modify it.

TEST

Where do you stand on the rigidity scale? The following quiz is based on various personality tests used to measure authoritarianism, dominance, and other traits that define the "uptight" personality.

1. It's hard for me to quickly adapt to change, such as a new job, friend, or neighborhood.
a. Rarely   b. Sometimes   c. Often

2. It bugs me when my surroundings are not neat and orderly.
a. Rarely   b. Sometimes   c. Often

3. I like to make lists of things to do.
a. Rarely   b. Sometimes   c. Often

4. I tend to feel dissatisfied or upset when I don't finish a task.
a. Rarely   b. Sometimes   c. Often

5. When on vacation, I get upset if things don't go as planned.
a. Rarely   b. Sometimes   c. Often

6. When someone takes advantage of me, it bothers me for a long time.
a. Rarely   b. Sometimes   c. Often

7. I tend to store used or old things since they may be useful someday.
a. Rarely   b. Sometimes   c. Often

8. I become uncomfortable when people don't replace things the way I left them.
a. Rarely   b. Sometimes   c. Often

9. I am strongly conscientious about fulfilling my obligations.
a. Rarely   b. Sometimes   c. Often

10. I am meticulous about caring for my possessions.
a. Rarely   b. Sometimes   c. Often

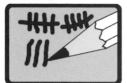

SCORING

To tally your score, give yourself 1 point for each "a" response, 2 points for each "b" response, and 3 points for each "c" response.

A score of 8–14 points: You are lax, laid-back, and a threat to no one. You may want to consider developing more self-discipline and structure in your daily activities.

A score of 14–19 points: You are generally easygoing, but you have your moments of verve and pluck.

A score of 20–25 points: You stand your ground, but you also give in now and then for the sake of smooth relationships with others.

A score of 26–30 points: You suffer from "hardening of the categories"—once you've made up your mind, nothing can change it. Try to learn to relax, develop more empathy for others, and be more open to new ideas.

EXPLANATION

Rigidity is influenced by one's biological makeup. Look at two babies. One may be tense, abrupt in its movements, and fussing for more comfort. The other is placid, adaptable to changes in light and noise levels, and generally content. The babies have different inherited temperaments that affect their personalities. The fussy baby will probably be more rigid in adulthood.

Aside from biology, most obstinance is a learned response to frustration. Much of it is based on fear. A rigid person's behavior is saying, in effect, "If things don't go as planned, I'm afraid it will be bad for me." They fear they will be unable to cope with the change. Flexible people, on the other hand, are less riled by change and adapt more readily.

Rigidity, which is more common in men than in women, is essentially a reluctance to trust others and to understand their points of view. Rigid types tend to enjoy highly structured work that calls for strict standards—they often work in science, accounting, the military, and research. At the other extreme are the more yielding types who shun protocol and organized ways of doing things. While the problems of being too uptight are evident, being too docile also has its disadvantages. People who are too flexible can be disorganized and lacking in self-discipline. Too much of either extreme, of course, is not desirable, and most of us can be found somewhere in the middle.

The best course of action would be to find that happy middle ground between a disciplined, organized standard of living and a freewheeling spontaneity. If you can figure out how to combine both, you will be able to reap the rewards that both personalities have to offer.

How High Is Your Power Motive?

The next time you watch a baseball game, take note of the manager. He is the power center from whom all crucial commands flow, and all eyes are on him. His use of power is constructive and authorized. But can you imagine if someone tried to give orders to a group that disputed his authority? Such a person would probably be labeled a compulsive tyrant.

Interpersonal power is the capacity to influence others while resisting their influence on you. Dozens of books are written each year on how to gain control and mastery over others. As a personality trait, power is neither positive nor negative—like fire, it can be used for well-being or destruction. When a mother stands firms with an unruly six-year-old who won't bathe, when a policeman directs traffic around an accident, when a teacher demands silence, that's power used constructively. The lust for power, on the other hand, becomes psychoneurotic or even illegal when one seeks to gain an advantage at the expense of others.

In his work at Harvard University, Professor David McClelland studied the power motive in thousands of subjects. He concluded that the will to power is a human necessity much like the need for recognition, achievement, or love. Over the course of his extensive studies, he identified three characteristics of people with a high power drive: they act in vigorous and determined ways to exert their power, they spend a lot of time thinking about ways to alter the behavior and thinking of others, and they care very much about their personal standing with others.

TEST

If any of the above descriptions sound like you, it might well mean that you are compulsive about having power over others. This quiz may provide some insight.

1. I strive to show competence in any group I join.
a. *False*   **b.** *Somewhat true*   **c.** *Very true*

2. I enjoy a job in which I can do things my way.
a. *False*   **b.** *Somewhat true*   **c.** *Very true*

3. I like to be the center of attention when with others.
a. *False*   **b.** *Somewhat true*   **c.** *Very true*

4. It irritates me when people try to dominate me.
a. *False*   **b.** *Somewhat true*   **c.** *Very true*

5. I don't take embarrassments easily.
a. *False*   **b.** *Somewhat true*   **c.** *Very true*

6. I dislike taking advice from others.
a. *False*   **b.** *Somewhat true*   **c.** *Very true*

7. It's important for me to do things better than others.
a. *False*   **b.** *Somewhat true*   **c.** *Very true*

8. I've always been good at selling others on ideas or a point of view.

a. *False*   ***b.*** *Somewhat true*   ***c.*** *Very true*

9. I like to ask tough questions that are hard to answer.

a. *False*   ***b.*** *Somewhat true*   ***c.*** *Very true*

10. At work, it would be hard for me to do a task that was meant for a subordinate.

a. *False*   ***b.*** *Somewhat true*   ***c.*** *Very true*

SCORING

Give yourself 1 point for each "a" response, 2 points for each "b" response, and 3 points for each "c" response.

A score of 10–14 points: You have a low power drive and are generally content with allowing others to control situations that involve you.

A score of 15–22 points: You have a more moderate power need and show flexibility in expressing it, and, at times, yielding to it.

A score of 23–30 points: You're motivated by a compulsive drive for power. Do you spend a lot of time wondering if others will "one-up" you? Do you find that people turn away from you? Try to get used to giving in to others once in a while. You may be surprised to find that an occasional nod to submission won't devastate your self-image, and it might gain you a few more friends to boot.

EXPLANATION

Since competition and the struggle to move ahead play such a significant part in our lives, many philosophers and behavioral experts see power as the most fundamental of all human motives. Dr. Alfred Adler, a colleague of Sigmund Freud, believed this. He discarded Freud's notion that sex was the primary drive in man and maintained that mastery over others was the main force in human affairs. As helpless infants, he argued, we develop an inferiority complex, then struggle all our lives to gain power in order to compensate for it.

According to Dr. Adler, becoming powerful is like reaching for an ideal. Some might argue that Adler was the first therapist to advocate the power of positive thinking. You might be tempted to debunk the idea that each of us strives for power when you think of a gracious, soft-spoken homebody, or an unassuming co-worker who simply minds his own business. But all people exert power in their own ways, whether it be through the determination to avoid contests with combative types, or in turning the other cheek in order to keep oneself out of a fray. Power can present itself in numerous guises, but the desire for it is indeed a universal trait that exists in degrees in all of us.

Can You Control Your Own Destiny?

We read daily about people who play the lottery and hit the jackpot. These happy occurrences are pure strokes of luck. Simply pick the right numbers and there you are, in paradise. Some people, though, have such a strong belief in luck that they will base important life decisions on it. This is far more risky than choosing a lottery number.

What governs the outcome of events in your life? Do you believe that it is luck, chance, or fate that actually determines what happens to you, and that there's nothing you can do to influence your life? Or are you at the other extreme, believing that your lot in life is mainly the result of your own actions and judgments?

TEST

Philosophers have argued over whether man controls his destiny or whether he is more like a pawn moved about by powerful social forces beyond his control. Take the following quiz to help determine whether you lean toward inner determination or outside influences.

1. When I am certain that I am right, I can convince others.

True   False

2. It's probably silly to think that I can change someone's basic attitudes.

True   False

3. Success in school or work is due mainly to my own efforts and frame of mind.

True   False

4. Whether I make a lot of money in life is mostly a matter of luck.

True   False

5. There's not much that a disadvantaged person can do to succeed in life unless he or she is educated.

True   False

6. Assuming there are two teams of equal skill, the cheering of the crowd is more important than luck in determining the winner.

True   False

7. Most problems work themselves out.

True   False

8. I sometimes get a feeling of being lucky.

True   False

9. I own a good luck charm.

True   False

10. It's better to be smart than lucky.

True   False

SCORING

To tally your score, give yourself 1 point for each response that matches yours.

1. *True* **2.** *False* **3.** *True* **4.** *False* **5.** *False* **6.** *True* **7.** *False*
8. *False* **9.** *False* **10.** *True*

A score of 7–10 points: You are highly inner-directed. You don't follow trends easily. You like your life to be in your own hands.

A score of 4–6 points: You have a balance between inner- and outer-directedness.

A score of 0–3 points: You tend to lean toward being outer-directed. This could mean you're discouraged about life, are quite young, or lack self-confidence. You rely too much on luck to determine your destiny. To build your self-confidence, perhaps it would be a good idea to set goals and give yourself credit when you reach them. In doing so, you will realize that you have the power to achieve results on your own, and that you do not have to rely on outer sources.

EXPLANATION

The subject of our quiz is really the "locus of control." The phrase refers to an individual's belief that he or she is inner- or outer-directed. People who are inner-directed, or "internals," think that they have control over what happens to them, while those who are outer-directed, or "externals," believe that they are at the mercy of fate or the power of others.

In 1966 professor Julian Rotter of the University of Connecticut originated the notion of locus of control. Since then, numerous studies have shown it to be a bona fide personality variable. Napoleon Bonaparte was a strong internal. He was a self-inspired and dauntless leader who refused to yield to outside circumstances. He once remarked, "I make circumstances."

Strong internals often have a take-charge attitude. They use their knowledge to alter their circumstances. Usually they are more optimistic and more likely to take action than externals, who see the environment as controlling them. Externals tend to be pessimistic about themselves and often do little to change their living conditions.

Rotter devised a test, similar to this quiz, which measures attitudes about our actions and their consequences. He concluded that these attitudes are largely learned from "significant others," such as parents, teachers, relatives, and siblings. For example, parents who are warm, supportive, and positive tend to produce internally-oriented children because they build the child's self-confidence.

Internals rely on themselves for their well-being and, unlike their fate-minded counterparts, assume that they can control their own health and safety. For example, they'd be more likely than externals to heed warnings to stop smoking, use seat belts, and practice effective birth control.

Do You Fear Success?

It's as inescapable as the common cold—the yearly tidal wave of how-to books that give formulas for becoming famous, powerful, and successful. But it's doubtful that these books work for even a few of the millions who purchase them. Why? Human nature. No matter how sound an author's advice, many readers will be blocked because they have a fear of achieving their dreams.

Books usually won't help a "success-avoider," someone who has a deep-rooted fear of achieving. But what is success? There is no one answer. The psychoanalyst Alfred Adler, a disciple of Sigmund Freud, once said, "What an individual thinks or feels is success is unique with him." For some, it may be a goal that is unattainable; hence, they don't ever feel successful. Rather, their lives are spent in continual dissatisfaction, striving for larger and larger prizes. These are perfectionist types who are rarely satisfied with themselves (or anyone else, for that matter). They are usually workaholics who compulsively strive to attain an impossible dream. Chances are good that they have an innate dread of ever securing what they seek.

TEST

Although each person's definition of success may vary, those who fear it tend to have certain perceptions in common. To learn if you might harbor a few of these negative attitudes about winning, take the following quiz.

1. I often feel superior to the work I do.
True   False

2. I habitually avoid being the center of attention.
True   False

3. For the most part, my success has been a matter of being in the right place at the right time.
True   False

4. I often feel uncomfortable or guilty when I compete with others.
True   False

5. I feel that people wouldn't like me as much if they really knew me well.
True   False

6. I often get a strange feeling, which I recognize as irrational, that everything could be taken away from me in an instant.
True   False

7. I frequently feel that my success was too easily achieved.
True   False

8. I feel restless or glum on a Sunday or holiday.
True   False

9. I have difficulty accepting compliments about things I accomplish.
True   False

10. Compared with my friends, I work very hard and play very little.
True   False

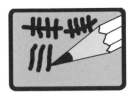

SCORING

To tally your score, give yourself 1 point for each "True" response.

A score of 0–5 points: You generally understand what it takes to get ahead, and are comfortable with the idea of being successful.

A score of 6–10 points: You tend to have stronger hidden fears of success than most people. Perhaps you are concerned that success would make you the center of attention, make people envy or dislike you, or saddle you with responsibilities you feel unprepared to handle. But as long as you manage success carefully, and stay true to yourself, your fears are unlikely to be realized. You may want to work on building your self-esteem, so that you'll feel better about getting ahead.

EXPLANATION

People who fear success often look down on the work they do, and see themselves as overqualified for their jobs. They feel that their success was not achieved by their own efforts. Instead, it came through luck or a good personal contact. To such success-avoiders, their achievements rest on sand, not a solid foundation built by their abilities. Often these people progress as high as the level of vice president but can't rise above it because of an inner insecurity about assuming total authority.

Dr. Leon Tec, author of *Fear of Success*, claims that anxiety about achievement is so universal it must be considered a normal human trait in competitive societies. One mistaken notion about fear of success is that it is less detrimental than fear of failure. Psychotherapists find that fear of failure is actually less harmful because it is a conscious fear, whereas fear of success is largely unconscious, and therefore much more subtly disabling.

Another mistaken notion is that all parents want their children to be successful. Case studies show that parents may unwittingly want their children to fail. Overly critical parents, for example, may take out their competitive frustrations on their children, unconsciously hoping their kids will fail so as not to surpass them. Martha Friedman, author of *Overcoming Fear of Success*, studied hundreds of these cases. She found that the fear-of-success syndrome starts early. Children who receive harsh criticism for their mistakes are likely to grow up fearing authoritative adults. For such youngsters, passivity is a way to cope with this fear. They throw in the towel and avoid the stress of assuming heavy responsibilities. Low self-esteem makes them unable to sustain the demands that are placed on them.

But can a fear of winning be overcome? Researchers say yes. Fear of success can be changed into a willingness to succeed in three ways: by building on existing strengths, by sharpening one's thinking about one's goals in life, and by coming to grips with any unconscious conflicts that interfere with these natural abilities in the first place.

How People-Sensitive Are You?

Everyone knows someone with extremely thin skin—a fretful type who gets nervous about how people will react to his or her actions. Super-sensitive people are acutely attuned to what others say and think. As a result, other people are quite guarded in their presence, fearful of unwittingly touching a nerve.

Supremely sensitive people are an extreme, of course, but we all share varying degrees of social sensitivity. This trait is called "interpersonal orientation." It describes one's awareness of others in a social setting.

Research done at Tufts University, in Medford, Massachusetts, by Walter Swap and Jeffrey Rubin, discloses some interesting facts on the subject. Over a period of two years they tested some nine hundred students and developed an interpersonal orientation scale. Some of the items on the scale are adapted for use in our quiz.

TEST

If you wonder how your social sensitivity compares with that of other people, take the following assessment.

1. I would rather discuss my personal problems with others than ponder them by myself.
True   False

2. I wouldn't ever buy something I suspected was stolen.
True   False

3. It is important for me to work with people I like, even if it means taking on a job that requires less responsibility.
True   False

4. When someone does me a favor I usually feel a duty to return it.
True   False

5. My friends and I seem to share the same musical interests.
True   False

6. I consider myself to be more forgiving than the average person.
True   False

7. I often wonder what a person sitting next to me on a bus or train might do for a living.
True   False

8. When I am spending time with someone, I am usually the first to reveal something personal about myself.
True   False

9. It seems that the more time I spend with someone the more I grow to like him or her.
True   False

10. If a panhandler asks me for money or food, it bothers me to say no.
True   False

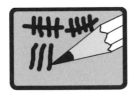

SCORING

To tally your score, give yourself 1 point for each "True" response. Keep in mind that neither of the extreme scores is desirable.

A score of 8–10 points: You are high in interpersonal orientation. The comments and actions of others affect your morale to a large degree.

A score of 5–7 points: You are average and in the desirable range with respect to social sensitivity.

A score of 0–4 points: You are low on interpersonal orientation and tend not to focus on the innuendoes of human interaction. You are relatively unaffected by others in the quest to achieve your own ends. You're probably a competitive, assertive person who has limited social needs.

EXPLANATION

The quiz is a social sensitivity scale. Each "True" answer indicates the presence of interpersonal orientation. Although some items appear unrelated at face value, the findings show that people with high interpersonal orientation levels feel the items on the quiz accurately describe them.

A person with a high score on this quiz is very aware of others. He is interested in and reactive to their behavior and tends to take their judgments personally. He is responsive to slights as well as compliments and, when rebuffed, gets moody and may sulk. He has more social anxiety than the average individual.

Sometimes, highly interpersonal-oriented people are not easy to deal with. They can be so reactive to others that they become very choosy in forming friendships. People with lower levels of this trait, on the other hand, are less attuned to those around them. They are more concerned with relationships that will promote their personal goals. They are not strongly influenced by the actions of others. They are usually drawn to "thing-oriented" jobs in such fields as engineering, accounting, and science.

What's Your Leadership IQ?

Have you ever yearned to take charge of a group, but were too shy to try? Do you recall the time you grew impatient with an authority at work, school, church, or temple, thinking you could do a better job than they were doing? You wished you could take over... but you didn't.

Thousands of books are written with the aim of coaxing people out of their reticence in order to help them emerge a winner in the game of life. But despite what the manuals say, evidence still shows that many potential leaders continue to linger in life's shadows and never give themselves the chance to carry the banner for their peers.

TEST

Are you ready to break away from the pack and lead the way? The following quiz will help to determine if you've got what it takes to be an effective leader.

1. True leaders are born, not made.

True   False

2. If I take on a leadership role, I'll improve my popularity.

True   False

3. The very best leaders know the value of keeping a low profile.

True   False

4. If you usually get along well with those in charge, you will probably be a good leader.

True   False

5. The best leaders always know what to do.

True   False

6. An effective leader must try to maintain a forceful personality.

True   False

7. My physical appearance has little or nothing to do with my becoming a leader.

True   False

8. I prefer reading fiction to nonfiction.

True   False

9. I usually stick to my decision even when it is unpopular with my group.

True   False

10. Being a quick decision-maker is an important trait of a good leader.

True   False

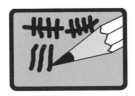

SCORING

To tally your score, give yourself 1 point for each response that matches yours.

1. *False*   **2.** *False*   **3.** *False*   **4.** *True*   **5.** *False*   **6.** *False*   **7.** *True*
8. *False*   **9.** *False*   **10.** *False*

A score of 8–10 points: You would be or are an effective leader. You are sensitive to the needs of those you would direct, and if you are not already in some type of supervisory role, you are probably not developing to your fullest potential.

A score of 4–7 points: You have an average ability to lead a group. Like most others in this broad category, you probably can improve your capacity to take charge if you receive some extra training.

A score of 0–3 points: You are a solid follower and not a leader of others. This does not mean you will fail in those endeavors you choose, but only that you will probably not achieve your goals if they have to be reached through others. People with low scores often work better on their own or as a team member rather than as a leader.

EXPLANATION

Read the following explanations for more details on what makes a good leader, and why.

1. *False.* The ability to direct others is not inherited. We can learn this skill just as we do any other complex task, although it requires strong and constant effort.

2. *False.* Once you've taken the helm, expect that others will have mixed feelings toward you. There's a kind of love-hate attitude that most followers have toward those who lead them.

3. *False.* Good leaders must make their presence felt. Studies at Maxwell Air Force base in Alabama found that keeping high "visibility" is reassuring to group members and fosters high morale. You can't be a lone wolf and lead the pack.

4. *True.* Managing, on the job at least, is a two-way street. To get ahead, employees must know how to "manage" their bosses. Management consultant Peter Drucker has stated that an aspiring leader should utilize his or her superiority "so that he becomes [a] resource for achievement, accomplishment, and … personal success as well."

5. *False.* If you make it to the top, don't expect to have all the answers at your fingertips. Even the most successful leaders have moments of utter indecisiveness.

6. *False.* In determining leadership ability, dominance is a less significant factor than intelligence and persuasiveness. Studies have found that the essence of leadership is interpersonal influence through effective communication.

7. *False.* Some of the world's most influential leaders were plain-looking: just consider Abraham Lincoln, Mother Theresa, and Mahatma Gandhi. It is true that initially you will garner attention if you are attractive, tall, or well-groomed, but it's your manner, charisma, and credibility that ultimately gain you a leadership role with others.

8. *False.* Those who are effective at directing the actions of others are usually factual types. They prefer to deal with material that is based on reality rather than on imagination. If they do read fiction, they prefer mysteries that call for a solution.

9. *False.* Being rigid won't gain you followers. A good leader is a harmonizer. Although it might be slower and more tedious, a good leader uses a democratic process to find out why others disagree with him. He then restates a position that is a compromise between his views and those of his dissenters.

10. *False.* Don't let it throw you if members of your group are faster thinkers than you are. Studies have shown that a quick mind is much less important in leadership roles than good judgment and the ability to carefully weigh all the facts before taking action.

Do You Use the Hidden Power of Your Wardrobe?

An experienced college teacher I know is convinced that her students are careless about their conduct because they wear sloppy clothes to class. Her impression isn't based on scientific fact—it's just a hunch—but she just may be right. There's evidence that clothing not only influences how others see us, but also has an affect on our self-attitudes.

Studies done by psychologist Michael Solomon at Rutgers University in New Jersey found that when students were interviewed for a job, those informally dressed (in slacks, sport shirts, loafers, etc.) did not have as high an opinion of themselves as those more formally clad. The latter (who wore suits) came out ahead of their colleagues on a number of traits: they were more assertive, felt they had made a favorable impression in the interview, confidently positioned their chairs closer to the interviewer, and asked for higher starting salaries. Apparently, the notion of dressing for success is not a myth.

TEST

How much do you rely on what you wear to prompt success in the things you do? To find out how clothes-conscious you are, take the following quiz.

1. Your decision about what to wear is influenced by whom you expect to encounter during the day.

a. *Disagree*   **b.** *Agree*   **c.** *Strongly agree*

2. You get a psychological lift when you buy clothes.

a. *Disagree*   **b.** *Agree*   **c.** *Strongly agree*

3. What you wear sets the tone for your mood that day.

a. *Disagree*   **b.** *Agree*   **c.** *Strongly agree*

4. You would feel self-conscious if you dressed inappropriately for some occasion.

a. *Disagree*   **b.** *Agree*   **c.** *Strongly agree*

5. You consciously or deliberately change your clothes to boost your morale.

a. *Disagree*   **b.** *Agree*   **c.** *Strongly agree*

6. It's important to be dressed in the latest styles.

a. *Disagree*   **b.** *Agree*   **c.** *Strongly agree*

7. What you wear colors others' impressions of you.

a. *Disagree*   **b.** *Agree*   **c.** *Strongly agree*

8. What other people wear influences your impression of them.

a. *Disagree*   **b.** *Agree*   **c.** *Strongly agree*

9. How appropriate your attire is affects your self-confidence in any given setting, whether it be at work, a picnic, or the beach.

a. *Disagree*   **b.** *Agree*   **c.** *Strongly agree*

10. You would feel uncomfortable if you met someone at a party who was wearing the same outfit as you.

a. *Disagree*   **b.** *Agree*   **c.** *Strongly agree*

SCORING

To tally your score, give yourself 1 point for each "a" response, 2 points for each "b" response, and 3 points for each "c" response.

A score of 0–18 points: You tend to minimize the impact your clothes might have on you or those you meet. Maybe you rely too much on your strongest traits (such as intelligence or your sense of humor) and don't pay enough attention to your appearance. Your clothing can add to your success. Try to make more of an effort to dress smartly lest you become lax about your impact on others.

A score of 19–24 points: You fall in the mid-range. You pay enough attention to your appearance as is necessary to be presentable, but you don't spend a lot of time updating your wardrobe. You conform to changing styles, but usually only after they become fairly well-established.

A score of 25 points or more: You have high clothes-consciousness, relying on your wardrobe to enhance your social image. You feel sensitive about being out of style but look forward to compliments when you know you look good. Heed this caution: Though you have high fashion awareness (a generally positive trait) be careful not to depend too much on your attire to succeed with others. In the final showdown, they'll judge you by your character more than anything else. No matter what your score on the quiz, be aware of the golden rule of dress: Clothe yourself according to how you want to be treated.

EXPLANATION

Clothes reflect your personality. Some might consider clothing a sort of extension of the self for the outside world to see. In addition to giving some indication of personal preferences, clothes have a language all their own and can be a cue to proper role conduct. Some obvious examples of the garb that might influence our behavior are a police officer's blue cap, a clergyman's collar, an executive's power suit, or a doctor's white jacket—each of these articles of apparel is associated with a particular person who's expected to act in a certain way. If these articles of clothing can have such a significant impact on us, think about how your own wardrobe might affect the way others view and react to you. If you're not getting the respect you think you deserve on the job, for example, try giving your wardrobe an upgrade, and see what happens.

Do You Quit or Keep Chugging: How Persevering Are You?

Perseverance is the energy that drives the human spirit. It keeps the soldier tracking his target, the lover pursing his beloved, and the athlete moving toward the goal line.

Perseverance, like all traits, exists in degrees. Would you perform an action repeatedly until you finally achieved success? Would you spend half a lifetime pondering the solution to a problem? Such persistence has played a large part in the success of noted men and women in various fields. Take Thomas Edison, for example. In 1879, after several thousand trials in his search for the right filament, he succeeded in inventing the light bulb. Persistence was present to a large degree in the accomplishments of others as well, such as Madame Marie Curie, who discovered radium, Dr. Jonas Salk, who gave us the vaccine for polio, and Alexander Graham Bell, inventor of the telephone.

Illustrious scientists are not the only ones who have proved that tenacity is necessary to achieve our goals. All of us struggle with problems in which persistence may mean the difference between happiness and gloom, life and death.

Tenacity has been widely studied in college settings, where students must continually muster the will to meet the challenges of ever-mounting schoolwork. A number of Persistence Disposition Questionnaires (PDQs) have been devised to measure the tendency to keep trying. One such study was conducted by B. N. Mukherjee when he was a professor of psychology at York University in Toronto. The items in the following quiz are adapted from his research, which was written up in the *Indian Journal of Psychology*.

TEST

Do you rise to a challenge or call it quits? To learn what your persistence index is, take the following assessment.

1. Little can be gained by people who attempt to do things that are too difficult for them.

True   False

2. Compared with others, I hate to lose at anything.

True   False

3. The stronger the chance of failing at something, the less determined I am to keep at it.

True   False

4. I am known to be a stickler for fighting for my rights.

True   False

5. It's better to accomplish many easy jobs than to attempt a few that are very difficult.

True   False

6. Luck is an important factor in determining whether one succeeds.

True   False

7. Compared with others, I set high goals for myself.

True   False

8. People who get ahead work only with their heads rather than with their hands.

True   False

9. Regardless of whether I work for myself or someone else, there's no change in my level of ambition.

True   False

10. I procrastinate more than my friends when faced with an unpleasant job.

True   False

SCORING

To tally your score, give yourself 1 point for each response that matches yours.

1. *False*   **2.** *True*   **3.** *False*   **4.** *True*   **5.** *False*   **6.** *False*   **7.** *True*
8. *True*   **9.** *False*   **10.** *False*

A score of 8–10 points: You are very tenacious and work hard to achieve your goals.

A score of 4–7 points: You have an average degree of persistence.

A score of 0–3 points: You give up too easily! When things become difficult, try to stick it out. You may be surprised to discover that a little effort can yield results that are more positive than you'd imagined.

EXPLANATION

Persistence was found to be a bona fide personality trait by Dr. J. P. Guilford, formerly of the University of Southern California. In his book *Personality*, he calls it the "desire to succeed." It's connected to ambition and a compulsion to achieve. Persistent people usually have strong needs for recognition and prestige. They like to make things happen quickly, and they believe that making money is an important goal in life. They rarely bypass a chance to excel at something, even if it is difficult. Generally, they don't believe that attempting many easy goals is the same thing as striving to reach a few difficult ones. They also don't take failures well—when failure occurs, they often double their efforts to succeed the next time.

Luck or miracles rarely factor into the persistent person's idea of how success will occur—rather, they set high aspirations for themselves and then become dedicated to achieving them. Persevering types also tend to procrastinate far less than the average person, and exhibit entrepreneurial tendencies, working harder on their own than under someone else's command. The perseverance trait is commonly found in artists, who practice diligently to perfect their art, students who study hard (and tend to become over-learners, studying more than necessary to pass exams), and salespeople, who sell far beyond their quotas. Tenacious people are more likely to use their head than their hands whenever possible in tackling a tough job. Keep in mind that although highly persistent people aren't necessarily successful, most successful people are highly persistent.

Are You Too Pushy?

When emotions run high, even the most democratic and well-meaning among us may, occasionally, insist that others see things our way. But if you know someone who acts like this consistently, you may be dealing with an authoritarian personality—one who likes to be the boss and take charge. Psychologists have labeled such people "F" types, because the original tests of authoritarianism were based on traits of fascist personalities.

TEST

Could you be an "F" type and not realize it? Take the following quiz to find out.

1. I like people to be definite when they say things.

a. Disagree   *b.* Disagree somewhat
c. Agree somewhat   *d.* Agree

2. Incompetence at home or on the job irritates me.

a. Disagree   *b.* Disagree somewhat
c. Agree somewhat   *d.* Agree

3. I like to drive quickly.

a. Disagree   *b.* Disagree somewhat
c. Agree somewhat   *d.* Agree

4. I don't mind standing out in a group.

a. Disagree   *b.* Disagree somewhat
c. Agree somewhat   *d.* Agree

5. I am argumentative compared with most of my friends or co-workers.

a. Disagree   *b.* Disagree somewhat
c. Agree somewhat   *d.* Agree

6. I make up my mind quickly and easily when faced with difficult work decisions.

a. Disagree   *b.* Disagree somewhat
c. Agree somewhat   *d.* Agree

7. I am intolerant when someone at work does something I think is foolish.

a. Disagree   *b.* Disagree somewhat
c. Agree somewhat   *d.* Agree

8. I don't like to accept advice from others.

a. Disagree   *b.* Disagree somewhat
c. Agree somewhat   *d.* Agree

9. Compared with my co-workers, I am more critical of the way people do things.

a. Disagree   *b.* Disagree somewhat
c. Agree somewhat   *d.* Agree

10. If it were possible, I'd rather give a lecture than hear one.

a. Disagree   *b.* Disagree somewhat
c. Agree somewhat   *d.* Agree

SCORING

To tally your score, give yourself 1 point for each "a" response, 2 points for each "b" response, 3 points for each "c" response, and 4 points for each "d" response.

A score of 10–20 points: You possess few authoritarian traits, and probably get along well with others. Some people may perceive you as passive, however.

A score of 21–30 points: You possess an average degree of bossiness. You are neither a pushover nor a tyrant.

A score of 31–40 points: You are highly domineering and may want to ask yourself whether this is the type of person you wish to be. You may be gradually turning off others by being too pushy. You'll spot the adverse effects of your behavior if you notice greater friction between yourself and others, fewer invitations to meetings and other gatherings, and a rash of fading friendships. These are all early warning signs that you are coming across as too heavy-handed. It may be time to lighten up and graciously accept it when someone else has his way.

EXPLANATION

The preceding quiz was adapted from a study conducted by sociologist J. J. Ray at New South Wales University in Australia. He found that authoritarian people tend to feel that most of the quiz items accurately describe them. Such types have a cluster of traits in common: They are highly conventional and tend to be intolerant and even somewhat prejudiced. They also tend to desire power in order to secure a sense of elevated social status.

Psychologists R. W. Adorno and E. Frenkel-Brunswik coined the term "F-type" to denote an authoritarian personality. Oddly enough, highly domineering people are usually conformists who have limited imaginations. Being more "herd-minded" than the average person, they are submissive to authority and suspicious of groups other than their own. Overall, "F" types are not very trusting—because they see the world as menacing and unfriendly.

Autocratic personalities dislike ambiguity and indecisiveness and prefer situations and conclusions that are clear-cut, with no shades of gray. They are critical, impatient with perceived incompetence in others, and vigorously argumentative about their point of view. They seek to be served rather than to serve and dislike sharing responsibility in team projects—they would rather assume the full burden of a course of action.

"F" types usually come from rigid parents who make strong demands on their children to do things "just so." As leaders, they like to come to quick conclusions. They feel uneasy with uncertainty and tend to encourage dependence from their subordinates. Thus, those who struggle beneath authoritative types rarely develop individuality or initiative, but instead, learn to be passive and submissive.

CHAPTER 7

Thought in Action

Are You an Undiscovered Creative Genius?

A curious thing about creativity is that if you can relax and let your imaginative powers emerge, your creativity improves. Dr. Ronald Taft has called this ability to let go "ego-permissiveness." It is found in many artists and creative persons who know the secret of abandoning rules of logic for a while in order to permit inspirational instincts to take over. Brainstorming techniques used in advertising agencies are one example of this type of thinking. But some people can't manage this—they are just too rigid for unstructured thinking.

TEST

Can you "let go" enough to be creative? To find out if you are the ego-permissive type, take the following quiz.

1. I would like to be hypnotized.
True   False

2. Occasionally, I experience déjà vu.
True   False

3. I like trying to see shapes in the clouds.
True   False

4. I have had the experience of staring intently at something until it slowly (or suddenly) became very strange before my eyes.
True   False

5. Sometimes, while asleep, I carry on conversations with someone who enters my room.
True   False

6. I have had the sensation of "highway hypnosis" while driving or riding in a car.
True   False

7. I am often so deep in concentration that I fail to hear others who call me.
True   False

8. I often get interesting thoughts when I am half- or fully asleep.
True   False

9. I like to be engaged in several projects at the same time.
True   False

10. I crack jokes, laugh a lot, and am generally known as a humorous person.
True   False

11. I am resourceful when it comes to dealing with unpredictable circumstances, like the sudden arrival of unexpected guests, a switch in trip plans, or a spontaneous picnic.
True   False

12. I have a wide range of interests in a variety of fields, such as the arts, outdoor sports, books, and crafts.
True   False

SCORING

To tally your score, give yourself 1 point for each "True" response.

A score of 9-12 points: You are an ego-permissive person at the high end of the creativity scale. You would probably be happy taking part in tasks that call for this ability if you are not already engaged in such.

A score of 5–8 points: You have about average creative potential. You would probably be able to tap into it more if you let go and relaxed. If you push yourself to use more of your imagination and novel thinking you can boost your creativity.

A score of 0–4 points: You are low on ego-permissiveness and creativity, and may need some stimulation. Try to encourage yourself to look for the unusual aspects of a situation. Perhaps joining an artistic workshop or a group involved in imaginative projects will expand your creative capacity.

EXPLANATION

Quiz items 1 through 7 relate to an alteration of consciousness that experts call "dissociation." This semi-conscious state of mind causes us to leave the here and now, to disengage our brain from the demands of the moment.

This suspension of logic encourages our creative powers and has been called "regression in the service of the ego." People who can tolerate such unusual states of mind tend to be innovative thinkers. They are more imaginative, intuitive, impulsive, idealistic, and willing to take risks.

Quiz items 8 through 12 are based on the creativity research of J. P. Guilford, who directed a major study at the University of Southern California that yielded many important facts about human creativity. Guilford concluded that creative people usually have several irons in the fire at once, display good wit and humor, adapt to new settings and quick changes, and have a broad range of interests. He concluded that being creative is connected with the ability to overcome what psychologists call a "constraining mental set,"—it is the flexibility to diverge from conventional views and thoughts. Such "breakaway thinkers" are our culture's artistic contributors: They compose new songs, write novels and plays, and invent devices that make life easier and more enjoyable.

Is originality of ideas an inborn trait? Scientific data suggest that it's not. Rather, creativity is developed over time. If a creative child comes from a creative family, his unconventional thinking was probably encouraged by parents and siblings, and not inherited.

One might assume that innovative reasoning isn't something to be pushed or hurried. But this isn't the case in professional areas that require "originality on demand," fields such as advertising, public relations, and commercial art—employees can generate ideas even when they are pressured to produce. This shows that we can all prod our imaginations a bit more to bring originality to the things we do.

How Well Do You Know Your Brain?

Let's say you're trapped thirty feet up in a burning building. You find a rope with a note that says: "In order to reach the ground, cut this in half and tie the pieces together." But, you think to yourself, the rope won't be any longer if you cut and retie it! Most people might assume the rope should be cut in the middle because the instructions said to cut it in half. But if you cut the rope in half *lengthwise,* then tied it end to end, you'd make your escape.

This simple example demonstrates a basic point about faulty human thinking—namely, that assumptions often lead to incorrect conclusions. This is the subject of our quiz.

 **TEST**

To discover what you know about the thinking process and to learn how to use your brain to better advantage, take the following quiz.

1. The higher your IQ, the more flexible a thinker you are.

True   False

2. We learn to think logically through formal schooling and education.

True   False

3. Thinking is largely a matter of gathering enough information to make a decision.

True   False

4. We can train ourselves to reason intelligently by studying subjects like math and logic.

True   False

5. Educators, philosophers, and psychologists are more interested in thinking productively than are average people.

True   False

6. A person who is usually logical is a good thinker.

True   False

7. The greatest need for reasoning occurs when a problem calls for a solution.

True   False

8. Complex situations usually require more time to reason things out than do simple ones.

True   False

9. Thinking needn't always be directed toward a target or an action goal.

True   False

10. Good ideas will come to mind if one relaxes and allows thoughts to flow naturally.

True   False

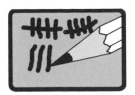

SCORING

To tally your score, give yourself 1 point for each "False" response.

A score of 8–10 points: You have a good grasp of how the thinking process works, and how best to harness the power of your brain.

A score of 4–7 points: Your have an average level of knowledge regarding the way the human brain functions, but could stand to learn more.

A score of 0–3 points: You have much to learn about the way the thinking process works. Read the following "Explanation" section to discover some facts about how the brain functions.

EXPLANATION

This quiz was based on work conducted at the DeBono Organization, a program founded by Dr. Edward DeBono that aims to teach thinking as a skill. An item-by-item explanation of the quiz follows.

1. *False.* The more intelligent you are, the more you'll tend to use your mind to defend a position rather than to explore it. This is likely to make you less flexible than someone with a lower IQ. Dr. DeBono calls this the "intelligence trap," and people with a high IQ must guard against this tendency.

2. *False.* Schools, for the most part, tend to be databases of facts. They convey the notion that facts are to be stored until needed. They teach what to think, but not how to think.

3. *False.* Most decisions are based on an average of only 30 percent of all information that's available on a given subject. Hence, in decision making and thought in general, reasoning and judgment fill in for an inevitable lack of total information.

4. *False.* Subjects like math have their own rules—they are closed systems. There's no evidence that learning the rules of a closed system benefits reasoning in an open one. Therefore, you should not turn to these subjects in order to learn thinking as a skill. Rather, you must deliberately focus on thinking as a separate activity without conflating it with a particular subject matter.

5. *False.* Studies find that businesspeople tend to be the most interested in thinking, because they are under constant pressure to produce greater profits. There are exceptions, of course, but generally speaking, people who are results-oriented are interested in thinking, because thought precedes constructive human action.

6. *False.* Logic is the second stage of thinking. The first stage is perception—the way you see a situation. No matter how good your logic, if your perception is biased by subjective factors, your conclusion will be inaccurate.

7. *False.* Being a problem solver is important, but it's only one type of mental activity. Sticking to this format alone deprives one of exploring new ideas, which could lead to more valuable and far-reaching generalizations.

8. *False.* Complex situations need not require more time to solve than simpler problems. What often slows us down is worrying about coming to a decision quickly. Worry can hinder your ability to think through problems in a focused and efficient manner.

9. *False.* To be most productive, all human effort, including thinking, should focus on a purpose, even if that purpose is simply to plan for future happiness or to have fun.

10. *False.* Relaxation occasionally yields good ideas but generally it is a way to avoid thinking. A small amount of tension actually sharpens cognition. Dr. DeBono has suggested that the best way to think is to focus on one aspect of a particular situation at a time, without concern about making a good decision. By breaking the task into smaller, more manageable steps, you avoid feeling overwhelmed. It should then be easier to put it all together in the end.

How Curious Are You?

nglish literary wit Dr. Samuel Johnson once quipped: "Curiosity is a sign of a vigorous intellect." But curiosity indicates more than just an active and productive mind. It's a bona fide drive just as much as hunger or thirst.

The curiosity drive is best seen in children who roam around a room, playpen, or playground in an endless exploration of their world. A contented individual in a novel setting will invariably explore his surroundings with more than just casual interest.

TEST

How inquisitive are you? To find out, take the following quiz.

1. If my partner is late, I'm usually interested in knowing the details of the delay.
True   False

2. When I come upon an accident, I usually ask bystanders several questions about what happened.
True   False

3. If I happened to pass the open window of a private home, I would probably look in.
True   False

4. I never open gifts that say "Don't open 'til your birthday."
True   False

5. I don't necessarily obey "No Trespassing" signs.

True   False

6. If someone ahead of me in line were wearing an outfit I liked, I would ask him or her where it was purchased.

True   False

7. I would probably listen in on a phone conversation if my line were crossed with someone else's.

True   False

8. I sometimes open other people's letters, or hold them up to the light to inspect their contents.

True   False

9. As a rule, parents should know most everything their children are thinking and doing.

True   False

10. A good boss needs to know what his or her subordinates are doing at any given moment of the workday.

True   False

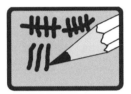

SCORING

To tally your score, give yourself 1 point for each response that matches yours.

1. *True* **2.** *True* **3.** *True* **4.** *False* **5.** *True* **6.** *True* **7.** *True* **8.** *True*
9. *True* **10.** *True*

Your score roughly indicates the strength of your curiosity drive.

A score of 9–10 points: You are highly curious and interested in the world around you. Be careful that you don't invade others' personal privacy in your quest to know everything that's going on.

A score of 5–8 points: You have an average degree of curiosity. You like to know what's happening around you, but may not always feel strongly compelled to find out.

A score of 4 points or less: You have a low curiosity drive. This may be the result of a high degree of self-involvement, a respect for others' privacy, or a general apathy toward what's happening

---

EXPLANATION

Curiosity is an ever-present human drive. Taking this quiz is a prime example of the endless interest we have in our own personalities and how to improve them. We may not realize it, but when our curiosity is piqued we build up a state of slight tension and discomfort. We relieve this tension by exploring that which is unknown to us. Anything new or strikingly different appeals to our sense of curiosity. Modern art, with its abstract and unusual shapes, has this kind of peculiar appeal.

Curiosity is an inborn trait in both humans and animals. Psychiatrist Harry Harlow, in his research at Stanford University in Palo Alto, California, demonstrated this when he supplied monkeys with a wooden panel bearing four metal latches that opened to nothing. The animals soon learned to open and close the latches even though they were not rewarded for doing so. In animals, curiosity can sometimes be even more compelling than biological needs. Experiments conducted by Professor

Philip Zimbardo, also of Stanford University, showed that hungry or thirsty rats often chose to first explore a novel environment rather than take time to eat or drink. People display similar needs to explore and understand unusual aspects of their surroundings.

We show curiosity in countless ways: toward people, toward nature, and toward ourselves. But at times, this unlearned tendency may work against us. It can be a disguised distrust of others, passed off as "harmless" inquisitiveness. It's hard to draw the line between healthy curiosity and morbid suspiciousness. If you're a super-curious cat with a high score, you might be non-trusting or doubtful of others' sincerity. You'll note that some of the quiz items query not just your curiosity, but also your level of suspicion.

If you have a high score, you might ask yourself what's behind your need to know everything. Do you lack trust in others? On the other hand, if your curiosity drive is very low, you may be withdrawn to the point of apathy or detachment, an equally undesirable trait that you should strive to change. Try to increase your interactions with others by sharing some of your thoughts and feelings with them.

Could You Be Hypnotized?

A number of years ago, the actor Zero Mostel needed surgery for a leg injury that he'd sustained in a car accident. For medical reasons, he couldn't receive the usual anesthetic before the operation and hypnosis was tried instead. The comic was kept comfortable in a trance, and the procedure was over within a few hours.

Stories like this one garner national attention and raise the hope of many who suffer from one ailment or another that perhaps hypnosis might work for them. But surveys show that only a small percentage of sufferers actually seek out hypnosis, because it still carries the reputation of being eccentric and somewhat occult.

But hypnosis is not as mysterious as many believe. The fact is, hypnosis occurs often in everyday living and only seems outlandish because we have labeled it as such. Each one of us passes through a momentary hypnotic state each night, as we go from wakefulness to sleep. You may recognize this "twilight zone" if you've ever heard a sound, like a phone ringing, and couldn't distinguish whether you were dreaming it or actually hearing it. Drivers often lapse into a dreamy mood on long stretches of highway, babies are lulled to sleep by rocking and humming, students daydream at lectures, and music lovers doze off at mellow concerts.

We are all amenable to hypnotic states. Yet skepticism about hypnosis still prevails. Perhaps this is because most of us first witnessed hypnosis as entertainment. We saw it as a sort of sideshow practiced by charlatans. But in the domain of dedicated professionals, it is a respected cure for such chronic problems as nail biting, smoking, obesity, and insomnia. It has proved to be an invaluable asset when life-threatening symptoms do not react well to anesthesia, and has improved such conditions as malnutrition, vomiting, uncontrollable hiccuping, and hypertension. What's more, it places no undue strain on the heart, liver, kidney, or lungs.

TEST

If what you've heard about hypnosis has piqued your interest, you may be wondering if you'd be a good subject. The following quiz should help provide the answer. It identifies traits of good hypnosis candidates and is based on research conducted at Stanford University.

1. I am female.
True   False

2. I am over fifty years of age.
True   False

3. I am above average in intelligence.
True   False

4. I am an original thinker.
True   False

5. I am emotionally stable.
True   False

6. I tend to be more of an optimist than a pessimist.
True   False

7. I am somewhat suspicious of the motives of other people.
True   False

8. I am relatively free of depression.
True   False

9. I have a good imagination.
True   False

10. I am a fairly independent person.
True   False

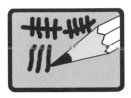

SCORING

To tally your score, give yourself 1 point for each response that matches yours.

1. *True*   **2.** *False*   **3.** *True*   **4.** *False*   **5.** *True*   **6.** *True*   **7.** *False*
8. *True*   **9.** *True*   **10.** *False*

A score of 3 points or less: You may be hard to hypnotize.

A score of 4 points or more: You will likely enter a trance without much resistance. The closer your score is to 10, the more likely you are to be a good hypnotherapy subject. If you would like to find a qualified hypnotist in your area, call your local psychiatric association.

EXPLANATION

Even if you received a low score on this quiz, it doesn't mean that you can't be hypnotized. Many people who are low on the hypnotizability scale are so deeply motivated to use hypnosis that they become excellent subjects for it. Read on to find out who has the easiest time falling under the hypnotist's spell. Each statement refers back to the questions on the quiz.

1. *True.* Females are somewhat more suggestible, and hence, more hypnotizable than males.

2. *False.* If you are over fifty years old, you are less likely to be hypnotized, since susceptibility to hypnosis diminishes as you age.

3. *True.* Intelligence is correlated with hypnotizability.

4. *False.* Conventional thinkers—rather than "break away" original thinkers—make the best hypnosis clients.

5. *True.* People who are unstable are usually harder to hypnotize.

6. *True.* Those with a cheerful, uplifting attitude about life usually respond best to hypnosis.

7. *False.* A trance-like state is difficult to achieve with persons who are overly cautious about the world and those around them.

8. *True.* People who struggle with depression usually need more pre-hypnotic conditioning than those who are happy.

9. *True.* If you have an active imagination, you're more likely to do well in hypnosis.

10. *False.* Independent-minded individuals often do not make good hypnosis subjects. One must be somewhat willing to depend on others in order to be a good candidate.

How Far Does Your Imagination Stretch?

Ralph Waldo Emerson once said: "The quality of the imagination is to flow, and not to freeze." Imagination, the ability to visualize things in our mind's eye, is a fundamental part of mental life. It is crucial not just in creating works of art, but in anticipating situations and in problem-solving. It's a fanciful way of going beyond the here and now.

Christopher Columbus had to imagine the world as round before he set out on his epic voyage of discovery. And Albert Einstein, who once remarked, "I rarely think in words at all," had to imagine a universe where everything is relative before he theorized about the relativity of space and time.

But imagination varies from person to person. Like Einstein, some of us think almost exclusively in mental images while others think in words. In fact, about three out of every ten people would probably have trouble forming a mental image in any situation.

TEST

If you've never had your imagination tested, or would like to test it again, take the following quiz. It is based on several imagination tests, including one developed at Yale University.

1. I can tell a white lie without becoming flustered.
a. Rarely   *b. Sometimes*   *c. Often*

2. I cry at the movies.
a. Rarely   *b. Sometimes*   *c. Often*

3. I can visualize patterns and images in clouds, mountains, wallpaper patterns, etc.
a. Rarely   *b. Sometimes*   *c. Often*

4. I get ideas that I think would make a good movie or book.
a. Rarely   *b. Sometimes*   *c. Often*

5. When I retell a story, I tend to embellish it somewhat in order to make it more interesting.
a. Rarely   *b. Sometimes*   *c. Often*

6. I vividly imagine extreme life situations, such as being stranded on a deserted island, or winning the lottery.
a. Rarely   *b. Sometimes*   *c. Often*

7. I worry about a possible accident when someone who is usually punctual is very late.
a. Rarely   *b. Sometimes*   *c. Often*

8. I enjoy abstract art.
a. Rarely   *b. Sometimes*   *c. Often*

9. I like to read fiction or stories about the supernatural.
a. Rarely   *b. Sometimes*   *c. Often*

10. When I awaken from a vivid dream it takes me a few seconds to return to reality.
a. Rarely   *b. Sometimes*   *c. Often*

SCORING

To tally your score, give yourself 1 point for each "a" response, 2 points for each "b" response, and 3 points for each "c." People with active imaginations tend to respond to many of the items with an answer of "Often."

A score of 10–15 points: You're a concrete thinker based in reality. While it is not impossible for you to imagine situations, you prefer a practical, realistic approach to life. You would benefit from stretching your imagination. Perhaps taking a course in creative writing or art will expand your way of thinking and boost your imaginative skills.

A score of 16–23 points: You have an average level of imagination. A balance between practicality and creativity allows you to actualize your ideas and see your fantasies take flight.

A score of 24–30 points: You have a very active imagination. It is a powerful force within you, but be careful to keep it somewhat in check to avoid becoming impractical. If your creative mind already runs wild, try to control it somewhat by being more practical and conservative in your daily decision-making.

EXPLANATION

Human imagination has excited the interest of psychologists since the early 1950s. Experts are now confident that it plays a key role in mental health. There is evidence that those who have difficulty visualizing scenarios or who are discouraged from using their imagination productively tend to become rigid or insecure, and often display various symptoms of neurosis.

Still, an overactive imagination can also be problematic—it can put you out of touch with reality and create difficulties in dealing with responsibility. Researchers believe that a distinct advantage exists for behavior-therapy patients who can form mental images. Imagination is often at the core of treatments for phobia, obsessions, and bad habits. In these situations, patients are asked to imagine those things that cause them anxiety or create other problems for them. They are then taught to relax while still imagining the distressing situation or object.

Do imaginative people have more fun? Probably. They tend to enrich their experiences through creative thinking. Witness the child who receives a new toy and gets almost as much joy out of playing with the box as with the toy itself. The child imagines the box as any number of things and incorporates it into play fantasies.

If your imagination index is fairly low, take heart. Studies show that imagination can be improved. The imaginative powers of children can be strengthened and expanded through a series of games and play exercises. Surely, adults can broaden their minds in a similar fashion—by engaging in activities that require them to think about and perceive the world in new and unusual ways. California psychologist Dr. Richard DeMille's work has verified this. DeMille's interest in imagination may well have been stimulated by his father, Cecil B. DeMille, the famous movie director.

Can You Judge Someone Else's Smarts?

Were you ever surprised by the dumb behavior of someone you judged to be smart? For most of us, intelligence is a trait taken for granted. But there's much more to the matter (and gray matter) than you might think. Brain power is a much misunderstood part of our total personality. Everyday, scientists discover new facts about what affects mental processes—and some of their findings may surprise you.

TEST

To test your knowledge of smarts, take the following quiz.

1. A high forehead is a sign of a high IQ.
True   False

2. The oldest sibling in a family tends to have a higher IQ than the children born after him.
True   False

3. Girls score higher than boys on IQ tests.
True   False

4. Intelligence has little to do with health, job success, or mental and social development.
True   False

5. If a person is creative, chances are that he or she is also intelligent.
True   False

6. Slow learners have better recall than fast learners.
True   False

7. Premature babies tend to develop IQs that are below average.
True   False

8. The time of year in which you were born has a bearing on how smart you are.
True   False

9. Since we think with our brain, improving the condition of our muscles won't improve our thinking.
True   False

10. You can stimulate your mental activity if you drink a little alcohol.
True   False

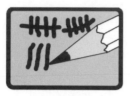

SCORING

To tally your score, give yourself 1 point for each response that matches yours.

1. *False* **2.** *True* **3.** *False* **4.** *False* **5.** *False* **6.** *False* **7.** *False*
8. *True* **9.** *False* **10.** *False*

The quiz is based on clinical and experimental research. If you get at least 6 correct, you are a good judge of human intelligence. If you score 5 or less, you probably have some old-fashioned notions about what can influence mental ability and, chances are, you are misjudging the brain power of those around you.

EXPLANATION

Read on for more detailed explanations of how you can learn to judge another's intelligence.

1. *False.* Many people believe this is true because they think a high forehead suggests a big brain. But craniometry studies show no correlation between brain size and IQ.

2. *True.* Analysis of thousands of adolescents showed that IQs decrease from first to last born. No one really knows why. Some experts say the first-born benefits from better prenatal development. Others believe their IQs develop more fully because first-borns have their parents to themselves longer than their later-born siblings do.

3. *False.* On overall tests of mental abilities, boys score slightly higher than girls. But the differences tend to disappear with maturity.

4. *False.* Psychologist Lewis Terman conducted follow-up studies of thousands of children and found that the higher one's IQ, the better one's health, social and mental adjustment, and job success.

5. *False.* Creative ability does not depend on intelligence. In fact, one researcher found that there was no relationship between scientists' creativity and their intelligence scores.

6. *False.* There are two significant reasons that slow learners remember less than fast learners. Slow learners usually have lower IQs to begin with, and therefore, have less memory capacity. They also take longer to learn because they have decreased comprehension—people best remember things that they understand.

7. *False.* Although premature babies begin life with perceptual and mental reactions that are somewhat below average, they do catch up as they grow to normal size.

8. *True.* The season of your birth does affect your IQ. Psychologists Florence Goodenough and

Clarence Mills, in independent studies, found that children born in summer average slightly higher IQs than those born in other seasons. They theorize that fetal brain development is better in the colder months.

9. *False.* Increased muscle tone improves the quality of our mental functions. Furthermore, some slight muscle tension facilitates learning. However, fatigue or too much tension interferes with our learning ability and judgment.

10. *False.* Alcohol, even in the most minute amount, is a neural depressant. Although it promotes muscular relaxation by inhibiting certain nerve centers, it retards reaction time as well as brain functions.

Are You a Creative Problem-Solver?

Remember Rubik's Cube? Did it keep you up at night? That confounding object is similar to the devices used in studies of problem-solving ability. Scientists have found that the ability to complete puzzles, as well as perform other mental tasks, is based on a set of learned skills. And the degree of our problem-solving skills does vary.

Much of the world's frustration, hostility, and discouragement is due to inadequate problem-solving skills. Most public schools do not teach these skills. With any luck, we may witness an introduction of problem-solving courses into school curricula the world over.

TEST

Many of us fall into traps when seeking suitable answers to the conflicts and difficulties of daily living. To assess your problem-solving skills, try the following quiz.

1. Most problems solve themselves in one way or another.
True **False**

2. I'm known to be a perfectionist when it comes to dealing with problems.
True **False**

3. It's usually true that the first answer that comes to mind is the correct one.
True **False**

4. I often shelve vexing problems in the hope that a solution will turn up.
True **False**

5. I often become rattled by tough problems.
True **False**

6. I often let others make decisions for me.
True **False**

7. I would prefer a job where I didn't have the burden of making tough decisions.

True   False

8. I've never been able to judge how well I've done on an exam.

True   False

9. To be honest, it's hard for me to admit that a solution of mine isn't working out well.

True   False

10. I have difficulty accepting a solution from someone who is younger than me or whom I consider to be below my competence level.

True   False

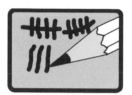

SCORING

To tally your score, give yourself 1 point for each correct response. Items 1 and 4 through 10 are false; items 2 and 3 are true.

A score of 7–10 points: You are a good problem-solver and, indeed, one to call when a resolution to an issue is needed. You view situations clearly and seek out logical solutions.

A score of 4–6 points: Your problem-solving skills are average. You may need to brush up on your ability to really look at a situation from every angle before coming to a conclusion.

A score of 0–3 points: Your problem-solving skills are rather weak. You probably rely too much on assumptions and intuition instead of examining the facts. Make sure you gather as many facts as possible before making a decision or jumping to a conclusion.

EXPLANATION

Researchers studied how we arrive at solutions and found that many people fall into traps and bad habits when it comes to problem-solving. Many of us have strong tendencies to bury our heads in the sand when facing difficult situations, a behavior known in psychological circles as "magical thinking." Our puzzling-out abilities are also endangered by what is called a "mental set"—a one-sided outlook that destroys the flexibility that should enable us to untangle complex or unusual quandaries.

This problem fixity can hamper us when dealing with human-relations conflicts, and it plays itself out in a number of ways. Some familiar examples are the child who avoids potential playmates because he feels he will be rejected, the boss who assumes that sick days taken on Fridays or Mondays are the means for an employee to prolong a weekend, or a student who assumes his professor will be miffed if he complains about a low grade. A mind-set that prevents us from confronting our untested assumptions in reality only prevents us from discovering the truth.

Note: To further test if you fall prey to a mental set, try to create four triangles using six matchsticks—without overlapping. The solution is given below.

Solution: The key is to think in three dimensions, not two. **Make a flat triangle, then stand the remaining three matches on top of it, like a pyramid, to create four triangles.**

Do You Live in the Perfect Tense?

Any reasonable soul knows that no one is perfect, right? Wrong! There are die-hards among us who strive for perfection with the belief that such a happy state is entirely attainable. But, to quote poet Alexander Pope, "Whoever thinks a faultless piece to see, thinks what ne'er was, nor is, nor e'er shall be." Perfectionists are playing a game that cannot be won. Of course, striving for the best isn't a negative activity. It only becomes a problem when it strains our relationships with others and when it runs us, exhausted, into the ground.

Studies show that "unsatisfy-ables" are compulsive people who become entangled in details. They suffer from what psychoanalyst Karen Horney has called the "tyranny of the should," an attitude that they should have done better at anything they attempted to do.

TEST

Do you have perfectionist tendencies? The following quiz might tell.

1. After I finish a challenging job I feel a letdown.
a. Disagree   *b.* Agree somewhat
c. Strongly agree

2. If I can't do a thing well, I usually won't do it at all.
a. Disagree   *b.* Agree somewhat
c. Strongly agree

3. Even if I could get away with it, I still couldn't knowingly allow errors to remain in my work.
a. Disagree   *b.* Agree somewhat
c. Strongly agree

4. On the bus, at parties, in stores, and in other public places, I catch myself critically sizing up strangers' looks, dress, or grooming.
a. Disagree   *b.* Agree somewhat
c. Strongly agree

5. I feel ashamed when I appear weak or foolish to others.
a. Disagree   *b.* Agree somewhat
c. Strongly agree

6. My parents were hard to please and generally critical of me.
a. Disagree   *b.* Agree somewhat
c. Strongly agree

7. I am unsatisfied if I only do an average job.
a. Disagree   *b.* Agree somewhat
c. Strongly agree

8. As a student, I was never really content with my grades.
a. Disagree   *b.* Agree somewhat
c. Strongly agree

9. I'm a compulsive type of person—I like to be neat, exact, and organized.

a. *Disagree* **b.** *Agree somewhat*
c. *Strongly agree*

10. I usually feel uncomfortable revealing my shortcomings, even to close friends and relatives.

a. *Disagree* **b.** *Agree somewhat*
c. *Strongly agree*

11. I would feel a strong urge to level a slightly tilted hanging picture.

a. *Disagree* **b.** *Agree somewhat*
c. *Strongly agree*

12. It would bother me if I had to postpone a job that I had already started.

a. *Disagree* **b.** *Agree somewhat*
c. *Strongly agree*

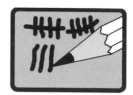

SCORING

To tally your score, give yourself 1 point for each "a" response, 2 points for each "b" response, and 3 points for each "c" response.

A score of 12–19: You are laid-back and do not generally feel pulled by perfectionist tendencies.

A score of 20–28: Your drive for perfection is average—you're not totally laid-back, but neither are you always a fuss-budget about details.

A score of 29–36: Watch out, mellow types! You strive constantly for perfection and are often uncomfortable when things are not "just so." Your perfectionist tendencies may make more laid-back types a little uneasy.

EXPLANATION

Dr. David D. Burns is a leading authority on this subject. In his work, at the University of Pennsylvania School of Medicine, Burns found that perfectionists use "all or nothing" thinking: They can't readjust their performance standards even when there's plenty of leeway to do so. They have difficulty relishing the fruits of their (or anyone else's) labor—only flawless results will fly. Perfectionists often live by the credo, "No pain, no gain." This unrelenting attitude makes them the fastidious, nitpicking picture straighteners among us.

The truth is that perfectionism is a projection of how such types feel about themselves—incomplete, imperfect, and inviting of criticism unless they hit the bull's-eye every time. An interesting finding shows that all this striving may not get perfectionists any farther than the average person—often people who stop at nothing to be flawless end up paying the price mentally and emotionally. Read on for more detailed explanations about perfectionist tendencies as they relate to each quiz item.

1. Perfectionists often feel a kind of anti-climactic, downcast feeling after they have expended much energy and drive on a job.

2. People who strive for perfection do not take failures well. Often they will not attempt to do something if there is a possibility of doing it poorly.

3. Perfectionists are deeply concerned about flaws in their work. They often spend inordinate amounts of time checking for errors before handing in an assignment.

4. People who have extremely high standards for themselves often rate others on a similar scale and see them from a critical point of view.

5. As hard as perfectionists are on themselves, they are very sensitive to evaluation by others.

6. Parents who are overly demanding and can't tolerate even slight deviations from their high standards often raise over-strivers.

7. Perfectionists have trouble accepting anything they do as "just average."

8. As adults, perfectionists often report that they could have done better in their school years.

9. An obsessive-compulsive personality is one component of perfectionism.

10. Those who aim to be perfect often have "disclosure anxiety"—they find it painful to reveal their weaknesses to anyone.

11. People with perfectionist tendencies are uncomfortable when things are askance or askew.

12. Perfectionists do not feel satisfied with loose ends or half-finished tasks. They have all-or-nothing attitudes, and strive for closure in whatever they do.

How Flexible Is Your Mental Muscle?

Have you ever had an argument with someone who, in the face of facts, still refused to change his opinion? It's possible you were dealing with a rigid person. But on the other hand, your adversary could have easily concluded that you were rigid, too. You may perceive yourself as a flexible thinker, but could it be that you're stuck in a mental rut?

TEST

To learn if you have "hardening of the categories," take the following assessment.

1. Compared with other children, I received more physical scolding when I was young.
True   False

2. Most people just don't care much about what happens to others.
True   False

3. Everyone determines his or her own fate.
True   False

4. If a group's members disagree amongst themselves, it is probably a healthy sign.
True   False

5. I believe in the old adage, "Eat, drink, and be merry, for tomorrow we may die."
True   False

6. It is not worth sacrificing your life to become a hero.
True   False

7. It's a myth that there is only one true religious faith.
True   False

8. It's possible to live a really full life without believing in any great cause.
True   False

9. My parents held very definite ideas about right and wrong.
True   False

10. Most people just don't know what's best for them.
True   False

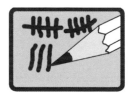

SCORING

To tally your score, give yourself 1 point for each response that matches yours.

1. *True*   **2.** *True*   **3.** *True*   **4.** *False*   **5.** *False*   **6.** *False*   **7.** *False*
8. *False*   **9.** *True*   **10.** *True*

A score of 0–3 points: You are a flexible thinker and are strongly accepting of others' attitudes. You are liberal in dealing with most issues and have a live-and-let-live outlook.

A score of 4–7 points: You are like the vast majority of thinkers. You have certain strong convictions but are flexible enough to keep a receptive frame of mind about the opinions of others.

A score of 8–10 points: You are closed-minded. Do you often get into scrapes with others? Your rigidity may make it difficult for you to get along with others, and may prevent you from understanding alternate points of view. Try to be more open to attitudes that differ from your own.

EXPLANATION

Inflexible people need a strong, absolute authority over their lives. They believe that might makes right, and that there are definite solutions to life's problems.

Social psychologist Milton Rokeach, author of *The Open and Closed Mind*, is an authority on inflexible personalities. His test, called a "D-scale," measures dogmatism, and is widely used in research on closed-minded people. The list of associated traits is quite long. Inflexible people are usually ultra-conservatives who resist change. They dislike indecisiveness and have little tolerance for even slightly ambiguous situations. For them, conflict over controversial issues such as politics or religion should be clear-cut and lead directly to a conclusion with no gray areas. Inflexibles are centered on their own viewpoints and as a result, can be emotionally unhealthy and socially challenged. The above-average hostility they usually harbor toward others makes it difficult for them to engage in the give and take so necessary for social harmony.

Close-minded people are typically intolerant of values that differ from their own. When they dispense justice to peers, subordinates, and children, they are likely to mete out severe punishments. But despite the fact that they wish to control others, D-types are also highly conventional in their behavior—they readily yield to pressure to conform to popular opinion and feel most secure in a structured, predictable environment in which they're a part of a majority.

The need to conform and control begins in childhood—parents who are severe disciplinarians tend to produce rigid children. A study cited in the *Journal of Marriage and the Family* reported that children with high dogmatism scores received more than the average amount of physical punishment from their parents.

What Are Your Dreams Telling You?

Sigmund Freud called dreams the "royal road" to the unconscious. As the foremost interpreter of dreams, he saw them as mirrors that reflect the reality within us even though, at times, they may be heavily disguised by symbolism and abstraction. For those who have tried psychoanalysis, the realization is clear enough: Dreams can suggest the absurdities in our lives, reveal the true motives behind our actions, and confront us with the paradoxes of our beliefs.

These nocturnal adventures are a barometer of our emotional lives. More often than not, people who have continuously disturbed dream patterns are afflicted with more than their share of adjustment difficulties. If you haven't paid much attention to your dreams lately, perhaps this is a good time to find out what they're saying about you.

TEST

To learn what your dream patterns reveal about your personality, take the following quiz, adapted from the work of R. Corriere and J. Hart.

1. I sometimes gain a better understanding of myself through a dream.
True   False

2. My dreams are generally pleasant.
True   False

3. I sometimes solve a problem through a dream.
True   False

4. I can recall my dreams at least twice a week.
True   False

5. I have the same dream about eight or nine times per year.
True   False

6. I have disturbing dreams or nightmares about eight or nine times per year.
True   False

7. A bad mood from a dream sometimes lingers into the next day for several hours.
True   False

8. I dream in color.
True   False

9. I cry, scream, or shout in my dreams about two or three times per year.
True   False

10. I abruptly awaken from a dream about once a month.
True   False

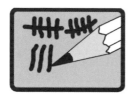

SCORING

To tally your score, give yourself 1 point for each response that matches yours.

1. *True*   **2.** *True*   **3.** *True*   **4.** *True*   **5.** *False*   **6.** *False*   **7.** *False*
8. *True*   **9.** *False*   **10.** *False*

A score of 8–10 points: Your dreams indicate that you are healthy and well-adjusted.

A score of 5–7 points: Your dreams are sometimes disturbing, but that need not indicate a grave problem. Perhaps you are trying to solve a dilemma while you are asleep, or you are preoccupied with some task that must be done the next day. For example, a nightmare about numbers may merely be your brain's way of reminding you that you need to pay a bill.

A score of 0–4 points: You may be grappling with a problem during the waking state, and because you are unable to find an evident solution, you try to resolve the issue during sleep. If your dreams are particularly upsetting, try to clear your mind before going to bed.

EXPLANATION

Scientists first began to study dreams in the mid-1800s. In 1900, Freud introduced his theory that dreams are the key to the unconscious. The theory revolutionized the world of psychology. Freud attempted to unravel the roots of his patients' neuroses by analyzing their dreams. Until 1953, little was done to study dreams scientifically. It was then that Professor Nathaniel Kleitman and his student Eugene Aserinsky of the University of Chicago discovered that a sleeping person's rapid eye movements (REMs) indicate that he is dreaming. Since then, numerous sleep clinics have sprung up around the world.

It is difficult to determine what our dreams mean because they are symbolic, and often we remember only a portion of them. But there are certain markers that tend to have general significance, and if you know how to spot them, they can help you interpret what your dreams mean. An item-by-item explanation of the quiz follows—it helps outline what you should look for in your dreams.

1. *True.* Dreams often present a chance to understand our true feelings about something which, in our waking state, may remain hidden from us.

2. *True.* A good feeling during a dream usually indicates that you are content.

3. *True.* Problem-solving in dreams is often reported by productive thinkers who continue to ponder a problem even in their sleep.

4. *True.* Generally speaking, those who can recall at least a portion of their dreams tend to have healthier personalities than those who can't.

5. *False.* A repetitive dream is a sign that the dreamer is struggling with a vexing problem or conflict and has not yet resolved it.

6. *False.* Dreams that produce strong emotion often reflect the dreamer's insecurities and fears (although some bad dreams do result from viewing something disturbing on television before going to bed).

7. *False.* Dream moods that last into the daytime indicate that the dreamer has sentiments that have not been adequately harmonized with the rest of his or her personality.

8. *True.* The tendency to dream in color suggests that the dreamer has rich creative and imaginative skills.

9. *False.* Calm dreams and sound sleep have always been associated with good mental health.

10. *False.* Freud taught that when we awaken abruptly from a dream it is because our internal "dream censor" has been unable to disguise its true meaning, namely, an antisocial wish.

How Do We React When Disaster Strikes?

It seems that the human race has inherited adversity as a condition for its survival. At 8:45 A.M. on September 11, 2001, a massive terrorist attack on the World Trade Center in New York plunged the nation into sudden anguish. Some 3,000 lives were lost and hundreds of people were injured. The world faced the ravages of the terrorists' fury. How did we cope?

Studies of behavior in crisis are not rare, but a survey conducted several years ago revealed some unusual findings. Nearly 3,500 victims of more than twenty-five catastrophic events—including the atomic bombings at Hiroshima and Nagasaki during World War II—were interviewed by the Federal Civil Defense Administration (FCDA) and the Disaster Research Group of the National Academy of Science. The survivors were queried extensively about their behavior during the crises and their responses were, at times, quite surprising.

TEST

The following quiz is based on the aforementioned study. Can you predict how people would behave when disaster strikes?

1. An overall reaction of mass panic is likely.
True   False

2. Disputes will arise about who shall assume a leadership role.
True   False

3. A rash of crime, particularly looting, assaults, and petty theft, will occur.
True   False

4. A significant number of people will break down mentally and/or emotionally and be unable to function.
True   False

5. The psychological after-effects last for years, even a lifetime.
True   False

6. People usually react with incapacitating depression and despair.
True   False

7. Problems with crowd control will arise when people flee the scene.
True   False

8. Victims commonly react by becoming more concerned with themselves than with others.
True   False

9. People tend to respond promptly to a warning that a threat to their life is imminent.
True   False

10. There is much disorientation, chaos, and physical affliction, all of which persists throughout the period of stress.
True   False

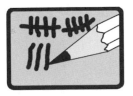

SCORING

To tally your score, give yourself 1 point for each "False" response. Most people answer 3 or 4 questions correctly. If you answered 6 or more accurately, you have an above-average awareness of how people would behave in a crisis.

EXPLANATION

It is difficult for most people to predict how they or others would react should they be faced with catastrophe. Here is an item-by-item explanation of the quiz, which should help shed some light. All items are false.

1. The FCDA found that mass panic is not a typical response to disaster. If emotional upset occurs, it usually centers on concern for missing loved ones, not the disaster itself. Children taken from their mothers during the World War II air raids in England were more damaged psychologically by the separation than by the experience of the bombing itself.

2. Groups do not remain leaderless for long. Our first tendency is to look for established authorities. If these people are not available, individuals will inevitably assume or be given leadership status.

3. Although catastrophe will incite isolated instances of anti-social or criminal behavior, it is much rarer or shorter in duration than is generally supposed.

4. Maladaptive behavior is a much less frequent response to disaster than is believed. When it occurs, it usually fades in a relatively short time and for the most part, survivors are docile and sensitive to the needs of others.

5. It is common to underestimate the resiliency of people who have experienced a great and sudden tragedy. Although some will develop "survivor syndrome" (guilt about having escaped while others died), most people will return to a normal lifestyle within a reasonable period of time.

6. The FCDA study showed that depression and despair, although present among survivors of a catastrophe, do not prevent sufferers from performing their duties.

7. Contrary to popular notions, movement away from a disaster area is usually significantly less pronounced than movement toward it. The National Academy of Science found that within minutes of a disaster, scores of people tend to converge on a devastated area. Participants in this "conversion action" are typically those seeking loved ones, those who want to assist, and curiosity seekers.

8. The net result of a natural disaster is often social solidarity. Sharing a common threat to survival produces a breakdown of social barriers and prompts spontaneous displays of generosity and caring.

9. Unfortunately, people are usually reluctant to heed warnings. They tend to disbelieve the gravity of a situation unless they have already been through well-rehearsed warning drills. It's estimated that no more than 25 percent of the population would take shelter within fifteen to thirty minutes of being warned about impending danger.

10. Although most people who endure a catastrophe suffer some transient emotional upsets such as nausea, diarrhea, or the "shakes," such reactions do not incapacitate them from responding realistically to the event. In fact, many rescues in disaster situations are made by the survivors themselves.

Are You an Unbiased Voter?

Y ou probably have a pretty good sense of your political views, but are you sure you are set for the next round of presidential or local elections? The true motivations behind voters' choices are worth their weight in gold. Studies show that people have many offbeat reasons for selecting the candidates they do. A politician is evaluated less often for his or her professional qualifications than you might think. And often people are elected by default—because they are deemed the least incompetent of the lot.

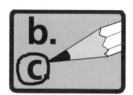

TEST

To see if you are truly plugged in to your political persuasions, take the following quiz.

1. A businessperson would probably do a good job running the country.
True   False

2. It's best to vote for someone who is already financially well off, because he or she will be less tempted to make money on the sly.
True   False

3. If a less-privileged person were elected to Congress, it would take him or her a long time to get accustomed to moving in such "high" circles.
True   False

4. The child of a banker or doctor would probably be a better president than the child of a laborer.
True   False

5. Only the well-educated are fit for the monumental task of running a nation.
True   False

6. The government would probably be a more honest institution if more working-class people were elected to office.
True   False

7. The country is best run by people raised in a political family.
True   False

8. It is not necessary for a president to be knowledgeable in all areas because he or she is likely to be surrounded by experts.
True   False

9. Our better universities probably attract the best applicants, and graduates of these institutions would therefore be the best politicians.

True False

10. We need more ordinary people in Congress—people who've led the sort of lives that most of us are familiar with.

True False

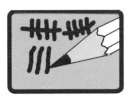

SCORING

To tally your score, give yourself 1 point for each response that matches yours.

1. *True* **2.** *True* **3.** *True* **4.** *True* **5.** *True* **6.** *False* **7.** *True* **8.** *True*
9. *True* **10.** *False*

This quiz assesses our political attitudes by testing our levels of "social deference." Oftentimes voters opt for those candidates who seem to be more knowledgeable or financially secure than the voter deems himself to be. This impression that the candidate is somehow "better" than the voter leads the voter to put faith in, and ultimately defer to, the people he supports.

A score of 8–10 points: You have a high level of social deference.

A score of 5–7 points: You have a moderate level of social deference.

A score of 0–4 points: You have a low level of social deference.

EXPLANATION

Your vote in upcoming elections will reflect how you feel deep down about who should be in government. A candidate's social class is a surprisingly powerful influence. Some political analysts have speculated that presidents such as Franklin D. Roosevelt and John F. Kennedy were elected because voters were favorably impressed by the wealthy upper class these men represented. This social deference was a more important factor earlier in political history than it is today, but it still prevails in the United States and, to a larger extent, in other parts of the world.

In Europe, for example, surveys show that voters are greatly swayed by office seekers' social class, which is probably due to the enduring tradition of aristocracy that's bound up with the European ruling class. One study, conducted by Australian sociologist John Ray, showed that European candidates from the upper classes were positively affected by their social standing.

Of course, one's social background does not determine his or her ability to govern. Class position is not the same thing as competence, and it's a risk to assume that they go hand in hand. Still, consciously or not, voters are all too often impressed by a candidate's social, rather than political, position.

How a citizen casts his vote strongly reflects his life circumstances. A person who is unhappy, financially strapped, or at a lower economic level is more likely to be socially deferent. According to the late Murray Edelman, former Professor Emeritus of political science at the University of

Wisconsin, people who lack stable and gratifying roles in life—such as satisfying professional or family situations—are especially vulnerable to persuasion. They are more likely to seek a candidate, usually an incumbent, to fulfill their needs. When considering potential leaders they look to someone who has established roots such as elevated social standing, strong finances, and a solid family background.

CHAPTER 8

Your Emotional Wellness

"Which of you gentlemen is the woodpecker?"

Are You Plugged-in to Life?

Sue had a bad day at work. It was one of those, "Stop the world, I want to get off" days. They happen now and again for most of us, but unfortunately some people feel this way all the time.

Sociologists call this condition "alienation," the opposite of feeling one with the world. A strong cynicism makes one feel gloomily pessimistic and distrustful of others' sincerity. People who feel alienated don't see themselves as part of society. Like Ebenezer Scrooge, they pull away and become embittered social isolates. Often they "tune out" through alcohol, drugs, and fantasy; for them, these outlets are the anesthetics for life's rigors.

A Gallup Organization youth survey found that one of the six major reasons teens resort to drinking is because it provides a feeling of escape from their problems. Such alienated youth often come from homes with firm disciplinarian techniques but weak displays of affection. Often the teens' parents themselves feel alienated from others because of a lack of social or business success.

People who move frequently may also develop feelings of estrangement. A recent study of eighth-grade children of United States Air Force personnel found that these less-rooted children projected a sense of isolation and felt different from other children who were more geographically stable. The mobile child has lower self-esteem and tends to identify more with adults than with peers.

If you have never really felt a complete sense of oneness with all of mankind, you're not alone. Few of us do. But the following quiz may shed some light on the degree of alienation you feel.

TEST

The quiz items are adapted from the work of Dr. John Ray at New South Wales University in Australia, who has studied alienation in all kinds of people from various backgrounds.

1. These days a person doesn't really know who he can count on.

True   False

2. Human nature is fundamentally cooperative.

True   False

3. In spite of what some people say, on average, the lot of humanity is getting worse.

True   False

4. Most public officials are not really interested in the problems of ordinary people.

True   False

5. It is difficult for people like myself to have much influence on public affairs.

True   False

6. Life is difficult and risky; the odds of finding success and fulfillment are largely a matter of chance.

True   False

7. When you get right down to it, no one cares much what happens to you.

True   False

8. In this society, most people can find contentment.

True   False

9. There are more rational than irrational people in the world.

True   False

10. Considering everything that is going on these days, things still look bright for the younger generation.

True   False

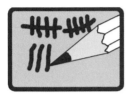

SCORING

To tally your score, give yourself 1 point for each response that matches yours.

1. *True*   **2.** *False*   **3.** *True*   **4.** *True*   **5.** *True*   **6.** *True*   **7.** *True*
8. *False*   **9.** *False*   **10.** *False*

A score of 8 points or more: You are more cynical and alienated than most people. You view others with suspicion, and generally like to set your course by relying on your own standards rather than those of others. You might consider reexamining your attitudes about life, either on your own or with the help of a counselor.

A score of 4–7 points: You show an average degree of identification with others. You feel enough of a connection with those around you to make you a happy, contributing member of society.

A score of 3 points or less: You are very traditional in your values and attitudes and not likely to be adventurous in plotting your life patterns. You are highly optimistic about life and feel secure in conforming to norms laid down by your social group.

EXPLANATION

Why do people become alienated? Famed Harvard psychologist B. F. Skinner, founder of modern behaviorism, called alienation a loss of faith, or "nerve." He saw the resulting despair as a sense of doubt or powerlessness in which people feel they can't change or influence their destiny. "They lack something to believe in or to be devoted to … these reactions immobilize men of good will," he said.

No one really knows how an attitude of alienation or cynicism begins. Some say it is socially derived, and that we absorb misanthropic attitudes from others. Freudians tell us that cynicism starts early in life, probably before age three, as a result of frustrated oral needs. Regardless of its cause, if one has a strong motivation to change, cynicism can often be reversed.

Young people who join cults are often thought to typify alienated youth. These individuals strongly believe that society cannot fulfill their need for security. They see themselves as different from those who lead conventional lives. But such people usually expect too much from the cults they join, and often find their way back into mainstream society.

Will Your Stress Make You Sick?

Tom ran out of gas on a drive with his family. His reaction was to fume and berate his wife for not filling up the day before. This is not an atypical reaction to stress. Some people might curse the car or be self-critical for not checking the gas gauge beforehand. Still others might view it all philosophically as an oversight that's nobody's fault.

The style we adopt in handling frustration depends on two things: our basic, inborn temperament, and the reaction patterns we learn from others. We can't alter the former, but as far as social learning goes, we do have some degree of control. The significant people we grow up with profoundly influence how we handle stress. Thus, the self-defeating coping pattern used by a parent can be assimilated by a child and eventually result in that child's breakdown of mind and/or body.

Since we all face stress, it wouldn't reveal much about a person to ask, "Are you ever (or how often are you) under stress?" The more telling question is: "How do you *deal* with stress?" Do people who use a stress-coping style like Tom's have a tendency to develop illness prematurely?

The answer may come from Johns Hopkins University in Baltimore, Maryland. In an ongoing study, Dr. Caroline Thomas and her associates have followed the lives of 1,337 students who attended the university between 1948 and 1964. The graduates have been given yearly questionnaires that ask about their lifestyles, and include questions about their eating, drinking, and sleeping patterns. Thus far the main finding, as subjects approach their senior years, is that their present state of health is related to how they reacted to stress during their earlier days. Dr. Thomas published a list of stress-coping behaviors in the *Journal of Chronic Diseases* that identified those headed for early illness.

TEST

If you've ever wondered whether your way of dealing with stress could harm your health, take the following quiz. It's based on Dr. Thomas's list.

1. I am a light sleeper.
True   False

2. I tend to be a forceful personality.
True   False

3. I believe that I am moodier than the average person.
True   False

4. I often become exhausted.
True   False

5. I often react with anger.
True   False

6. I tend to increase the number of my activities when I am under pressure.
True   False

7. I am more of a perfectionist than most of my friends are.
True   False

8. I usually don't pay much attention to my health.
True   False

9. When stress hits, I eat more or less than usual.

True   False

10. I sometimes feel nauseous.

True   False

11. I often get a strong urge to eat, drink alcohol, or smoke.

True   False

12. I generally feel moderate to strong bodily tension.

True   False

SCORING

To tally your score, give yourself 1 point for each "True" response.

A score of 10–12 points: You have a self-defeating manner of handling pressure and are among those most susceptible to physical or mental breakdowns. You overreact to frustration and wrongly place equal importance upon the outcome of large or small events in your life. You would definitely benefit from modifying your outlook on life. Perhaps a talk with your doctor or a counselor might help you accomplish this.

A score of 7–9 points: Your style of coping with stress and frustration is adequate, though there is room for improvement. You'll do about as well as the average person in managing tough situations. If your stress is prolonged and severe enough, however, you might suffer some bodily reactions that could make you ill. You could probably improve your health by adopting a more relaxed attitude toward life and its demands.

A score of 0–6 points: You react to stress in an efficient manner. You are not likely to break down prematurely, compared with high scorers on this quiz. In a crisis, you would probably maintain enough stamina and be able to call on your resourcefulness to see your way out of the dilemma.

EXPLANATION

Dr. Thomas has been involved with more than 100 studies of stress-coping styles and has found a strong link between stress and various ailments such as heart dysfunction, high blood pressure, and emotional disturbance. She also determined that the way in which one manages stress seems to influence the type of ailment that can develop. For example, those subjects who became very angry under stress were most likely to develop coronary problems, while perfectionists were susceptible to cancer. Those who were hard-driving, ambitious, and independent tended to develop stomach, heart, and digestive tract disorders. People with a rigid conscience and an unusually strong sense of duty became insomniacs and got migraine headaches, while insecure and sensitive types wound up with skin problems and asthma. On the brighter side, subjects with good health habits (those who were non-smokers, exercised regularly, and maintained adequate diets) tended to handle stress better—and were healthier as well.

How High Is Your Self-Esteem?

What is your most precious asset? Your best friend, your job skills, your creativity, the love of your family? Would you believe there is something even more precious than any of these? Think for a moment about your self-esteem, that cluster of complimentary feelings and attitudes you hold about yourself that could mean the difference between a sense of success or failure as a human being.

Your self-esteem is reflected in much of your behavior, and even an untrained eye can sometimes easily detect it. For example, how would you compare the self-esteem of a person who talks in a mumble and walks with a slouch to one who speaks in clear, moderate tones and moves about with head and shoulders held high? There are subtle ways to judge your self-esteem. One way is by examining the manner in which you deal with others.

TEST

The following quiz presents a list of interpersonal actions and attitudes that indirectly reveal what you think about yourself. Answer honestly.

1. I am usually comfortable and poised among strangers.
True   False

2. I am often jealous or envious of others.
True   False

3. I always accept compliments without feeling embarrassed or nervous.
True   False

4. I openly show recognition and appreciation when others do something noteworthy.
True   False

5. I can almost always accept disagreements without feeling "put down."
True   False

6. I strongly seek recognition and praise.
True   False

7. I am known as one who is hard to please.
True   False

8. I am often miffed if the opinions of others differ from mine.
True   False

9. I am sometimes embarrassed in public by those close to me.
True   False

10. I judge my worth by comparing myself to others.
True   False

SCORING

To tally your score, give yourself 1 point for each response that matches yours.

1. *True*   **2.** *False*   **3.** *True*   **4.** *True*   **5.** *True*   **6.** *False*   **7.** *False*
8. *False*   **9.** *False*   **10.** *False*

A score of 6 points or more: Your self-esteem is healthy and robust.

A score of 5 points or less: Your self-esteem could be stronger and needs a boost.

EXPLANATION

What is the basis for this essential element of mental health? Self-esteem is a personal, subjective evaluation we develop in childhood as we receive feedback from others concerning our behavior, school performance, appearance, and the like. From these appraisals we draw conclusions about our overall worth and value. A child who is made to feel proud of himself develops high self-esteem, while one who is constantly criticized tends to grow up with low self-esteem. Such people tend to be moody, gloomy, and unable to deal effectively with others. They tend to belittle the judgment of others and be overly critical. Sometimes, they are weak personalities who too easily follow the suggestions of others.

So when considering self-esteem, it's easy to mistakenly believe that if some is good, more is better. But this isn't the case. Too much self-esteem fosters a distorted appraisal of oneself, and exaggerated self-esteem is sometimes reflected in pathological narcissism. The right amount of self-esteem is a realistic amount. Considerable evidence within the past twenty-five years indicates that changing our level of self-esteem is dependent upon changing our thinking patterns. Psychotherapists like Dr. Albert Ellis and Dr. Aaron Beck have been most successful with cognitive therapy, a method that teaches clients to change their way of thinking about themselves. These new thinking patterns can replace old, detrimental ones and help to heighten self-esteem.

Are You a Worrywart?

Chronic worriers don't give up easily. There's the classic anecdote about the fretful wife who retorted to her husband: "Please don't tell me worry doesn't help. Most everything I worry about doesn't come true!"

The tendency to be vexed occasionally by life's stressors is such a basic part of the human condition that to never worry would probably be considered an abnormality by mental health professionals. Worry exists at all ages, in all times, and in all places. You probably won't find the term "worry" in most psychology textbooks, however; it's called "anxiety" instead, and it ranges from a disquieting distraction to a highly disturbed mind state.

Professors Raymond B. Cattell at the University of Illinois in Chicago, and J. P. Guilford, formerly of the University of Southern California in Los Angeles, studied the traits of the chronic worrywart and devised questionnaires to identify such types. The following quiz is based on questions similar to those they used.

TEST

To find out if you are apt to be anxious, take the following quiz.

1. I am considered by others to be serious-minded.
a. Rarely   *b.* Sometimes   *c.* Often

2. I think about my home when I am away from it.
a. Rarely   *b.* Sometimes   *c.* Often

3. I have trouble falling asleep.
a. Rarely   *b.* Sometimes   *c.* Often

4. When someone is angry or displeased with me, I don't forget it quickly.
a. Rarely   *b.* Sometimes   *c.* Often

5. Others would judge me to be overly conscientious in the things I do.
a. Rarely   *b.* Sometimes   *c.* Often

6. I dwell upon my duties at work or home when on vacation.
a. Rarely   *b.* Sometimes   *c.* Often

7. Compared to my friends, when I make a mistake it bothers me a lot.
a. Rarely   *b.* Sometimes   *c.* Often

8. When someone is cold to me my first thought is: Have I offended him or her?
a. Rarely   *b.* Sometimes   *c.* Often

9. When I leave home I return to make sure the door is locked, the stove is off, etc.
a. Rarely   *b.* Sometimes   *c.* Often

10. I have had significant changes in my eating habits.
a. Rarely   *b.* Sometimes   *c.* Often

11. When with strangers I feel I might be indadequate.

a. Rarely   *b.* Sometimes   *c.* Often

12. When I go for a routine medical check-up, I worry what the doctor might find.

a. Rarely   *b.* Sometimes   *c.* Often

SCORING

To tally your score, give yourself 1 point for each "a" response, 2 points for each "b" response, and 3 points for each "c" response.

A score of 12–15 points: You're low-key, easygoing, and fun to be around.

A score of 16–24 points: You're an average worrier, like most people.

A score of 25–36 points: You're a high-powered worrier. It would help to challenge your untested assumptions about the things that bother you. Keep a record of your specific concerns and see if they actually pan out as badly as you fear.

EXPLANATION

Worry is continuous, non-constructive thinking accompanied by fear. Chronic "dreaders" stew over most anything worthy of their attention. When piddling matters dominate a worrier's thoughts, it often means that they're struggling with a deeper, free-floating anxiety related to something more substantial, such as the possible loss of a job, potential ill health, or a lost love. Trifling worry will persist until this basic conflict is resolved. The free-floating anxiety is ready to attach itself to almost any incident—no matter how trivial—but the sufferer doesn't see this connection. So, if you advise someone "not to worry," don't expect it to help much, for those with deeper fears will soon latch onto some other concern.

Everyone worries: children worry over school and peers, middle-aged people over family and money, senior citizens about their health and safety. Surveys show that students worry a lot about passing exams. They also show that students who worry get lower grades than those who don't. Worry increases with age, and women of any age brood twice as much as men. But many of those tormented don't recognize, or won't admit, that they worry. Their ruminations have become a habit. Often, they unwittingly reveal their anxiety because apprehension correlates with other traits that are not easy to hide, like drinking, smoking, and overeating. Worriers are usually shy, indecisive, inwardly tense, and outwardly composed. They're likely to be socially inhibited and lacking in spontaneity.

There isn't yet a scientific explanation of worry. It's probably partly biological in origin and is related to our brain structure and its hormones. The tendency to fret is also a matter of social learning. A child with an uptight parent tends to develop anxiety and worry habits. Through imagery, cognitive therapists help worriers to reduce their anxiety levels and think more clearly by relaxing them and having them imagine the specific situations that prompt their trepidation. By coping successfully in their imagination with fear, worriers become desensitized and can ultimately be cured.

One technique you can use to help a worrier is to show that you truly understand how he or she feels. Expressing empathy is more honestly supportive than the false reassurance we usually dispense unthinkingly, namely: "Don't worry, everything will turn out okay."

Are You Addiction Prone?

Take three ordinary people: Judy is an efficient housewife, Cheryl is a college honors student, and Jim, a successful businessman. But look closer: Judy is a chain smoker, Cheryl downs twelve cups of coffee a day, and Jim drinks three martinis at every lunch. These "everyday people" are substance abusers, and there are many others like them.

In the United States, 13 million people drink too much alcohol, and more than 2 million people abuse drugs like Valium. Millions more overeat, smoke excessively, or overindulge in chocolate and soft drinks. Strictly speaking, although Judy, Cheryl, and Jim are not addicts, they do share some personality traits with those who are.

TEST

If you consistently crave something—even something as seemingly benign as nuts or pastries—and you wonder if you might have any of the traits of a full-blown substance abuser, the following quiz might tell you.

1. I perspire easily.
True   False

2. I enjoy reading newspaper crime stories.
True   False

3. I take more risks than most of my friends do.
True   False

4. I often satisfy my craving for excitement by doing something impulsive.
True   False

5. I was a discipline problem at school.
True   False

6. I suffer from bouts of depression.
True   False

7. When under stress, I tend to get headaches, diarrhea, or stomachaches.
True   False

8. I get restless and am easily bored.
True   False

9. I enjoy big noisy parties.
True   False

10. I often stole things as a child.
True   False

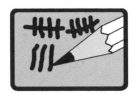

SCORING

Give yourself 1 point for each "True" response.

A score of 0–4 points: Your potential for addiction is very low. You possess few to none of the personality traits associated with addictive behavior.

A score of 5–7 points: Most people score in this range. You have some of the predisposing factors for addiction, but aren't likely to have any serious problems with it.

A score of 8–10 points: You exhibit many of the same traits associated with people who have problems with addiction. Be aware of your behaviors now, and seek out help if you notice any of your habits growing into full-time fixations.

EXPLANATION

The search to identify the personality traits that predict substance abuse has been a long one. But such types have certain traits in common, such as a high level of inner tension, excitement when doing or hearing about daring exploits, a propensity for taking risks, and an opposition to authority. Such high-risk types also share a history of mood swings, a tendency to manifest physical symptoms in relation to stress, and a feeling of generalized boredom with the ordinariness of everyday life.

The quiz is based on the findings of John Graham and Gloria Leon, whose work at Kent State University, in Ohio, and the University of Minnesota, respectively, spearheaded research to identify substance abusers. They studied thousands of substance-dependent personalities and found that they could identify about 79 percent of such types from a group of several thousand subjects. One of Leon's studies of a large freshman group identified with 85 percent accuracy students who became alcoholics thirteen years later.

Substance abusers are orally fixated and relieve their frustration through activities of the mouth like eating, smoking, and drinking (usually alcohol). This oral fixation is a prime trait of the addictive person, and is not found significantly in other people. Why some people under stress develop addictions instead of other symptoms, like compulsive hand washing or a physical tick, is unknown. Symptom selection can even vary within the same person who, at one time of stress may develop a headache or a stammer, and at another times, an addiction.

Do You See Clouds or a Silver Lining?

It seems all too common these days to have a pessimistic view about the future. But if we could turn back the clock we'd likely find many more optimists than pessimists—right? Not necessarily. Those pessimists really hang in there.

Even in so-called good times when most folks are heads-up and smiling, pessimists are still down-mouthed and gloomy. If you're getting the message that many people are just naturally on the glum side, you're absolutely right.

Human beings, of course, aren't easy to catalog. Most people will show some characteristics of both the optimist and the pessimist. For instance, even the gloomiest among us would show flashes of elation if he or she won the lottery. Similarly, a run of bad luck would dim the outlook of even the jolliest of optimists.

TEST

Whether you think you're basically an optimist or a pessimist, take this quiz, which helps predict what side you lean toward. However, if you already feel that you're going to get a bad score, it's probably useless to go further—you're a pessimist!

1. I always check my bill and count my change in a restaurant.

True   False

2. I rarely open a conversation with a stranger.

True   False

3. At work, I usually feel timid when with my superiors.

True   False

4. I believe my previous hardships have made me a better person.

True   False

5. I've almost never been accused of being aggressive or overly assertive.

True   False

6. I get the blues more often than most of my friends.

True   False

7. I don't gamble at all, or only for penny-ante stakes.

True   False

8. I've never arrived late for a scheduled airplane flight.

True   False

9. I'd rather keep my present job than take a risky one that pays 25 percent more.

True   False

10. I dwell on unpleasant experiences for a long time.

True   False

11. I do more listening than talking when with friends.

True   False

12. I worry more about little things than most of my friends.

True   False

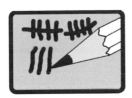

SCORING

To tally your score, give yourself 1 point for each "True" response.

A score of 0–4 points: You're a true optimist. You expect the best from others and from life, and often, you receive it.

A score of 5–9 points: You strike an average balance between pessimism and optimism. Your outlook on life probably changes daily depending on various influences, like your mood or the weather.

A score of 10–12: You are thoroughly entrenched in pessimism. You probably go through life expecting more than your fair share of disappointment.

EXPLANATION

If you scored low on this quiz and fancy yourself an optimist, consider yourself fortunate. You probably glide through life relatively happy and carefree. If, on the other hand, you scored high on the pessimism scale, read on.

Freudian psychoanalysts say that pessimism begins very early in our development, somewhere between infancy and three years of age. It most likely stems from unsatisfied oral needs like sucking, biting, and chewing. The result is a person who develops a personality that could be described as cautious, suspicious, fearful, long-suffering, or melancholic. Added up, such traits give us the pessimistic personality.

If this sounds like you, don't despair—there is hope. Try to force yourself to get out more and partake in some sort of constructive activity, like taking up a craft or joining a volunteer group. Make it a point to stay away from gloomy people and seek out more upbeat people with whom you've had a good time. In changing your activities, you can change your attitude.

Does Anger Get the Best of You?

W. C. Fields was once asked, "Are clubs good for children?" His tart retort was, "Yes, but only if all else fails." Fields's wisecracks, of course, were calculated to maintain his image as a rascal of social irreverence. His behavior was an effort to increase his box office profit, but some of us get bogged down with ill will as a way of life, feeling chilly toward everyone in general, and usually losing friends as a result.

But humans are not born mad or hostile; rather, frustrations usually cause such emotions to well up within us and incite problems. Animosity is directly linked to insufficient emotional well-being. Where do you stand? Do you have more than your fair share of ire to dole out? Take the following quiz to see if you're on the warpath with others.

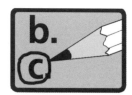

TEST

The following quiz is similar to those used to gauge social interaction patterns.

1. I am usually the one to stand up for the rights of other people.
True   False

2. It irritates me when peers or family members tell me what to do.
True   False

3. Expressing anger to someone who annoys you is emotionally healthy.
True   False

4. It bothers me very much to be considered "second best."
True   False

5. Most of the time, I am willing to fight for what I want.
True   False

6. I would have no qualms talking back to an authority figure such as a guard or police officer.
True   False

7. I like to direct the actions of others.
True   False

8. I probably would try to get even with people who had been bossy or pushy toward me.
True   False

9. If I'm upset with someone, I don't hesitate to let him or her know about it.
True   False

10. People will take advantage of you if you are humble.
True   False

11. A person who is spontaneous in releasing anger is better adjusted than one who is slow to express it.
True   False

12. I would feel quite glad if someone told off a person I found obnoxious.
True   False

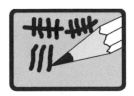

SCORING

To tally your score, give yourself 1 point for each "True" response.

A score of 0–6: You have an average degree of hostility that you'd be willing to vent toward others.

A score of 7 points or more: You have an above-average amount of anger and might do well to examine what's setting you off. It may be that the ways you're expressing your feelings are increasing your level of hostility. Chances are you'd benefit from a more controlled release of this volatile emotion.

Note: There is always a chance that the introduction to a test can tip you off to what is being measured, causing you to inadvertently slant your answers in a socially approved direction. If you fear this may have been the case, ask someone close to you to take the quiz with you in mind, then compare your answers.

EXPLANATION

Social animosity is so extensive, some experts used to view it as an inborn trait. But this belief has changed. Dr. Karen Horney, a Freudian disciple, maintained that anger is not an inborn quality but a reaction acquired through experience, especially with one's parents.

Horney theorized that humans have a built-in capacity for aggression, and it's triggered when one is faced with parents or caregivers who are indifferent, inconsistent, or interfering. A child in such a setting becomes reluctant to express his or her frustrations or animosity, so represses these emotions to a point where they stimulate feelings of guilt and unworthiness. This complex emotional web fosters a love-hate relationship within the child, which he or she resolves in one of three ways: by moving toward others (in an attempt to please or placate them); by moving against others (being anti-social or domineering); or by moving away from others (acting aloof or distant).

Unfortunately, there is no dearth of differing notions about anger, how it's caused and how it should be expressed. For example, item 11 of our quiz deals with how anger should be released in order to alleviate ire. Dr. Jack Hokenson addresses this topic in his book *The Dynamics of Aggression,* in which he summarizes studies that show that venting anger does not always reduce its ill effects. In fact, if people in conflict fail to deal with the root of their emotions, the conflict may only worsen.

Further, spontaneous hostility (which is discussed in items 9 and 11) is best quelled with restraint rather than expression. A study by M. K. Biaggio at the University of Idaho found that students who were quick to anger were less emotionally healthy than those who showed self-control.

People who respond "True" to the majority of items on our quiz tend to bear more hostility toward others than do those who respond "False." They are likely to be unfriendly, untrusting types with fewer social commitments. Among this group the level of self-sufficiency is high—these people tend to avoid situations in which others may be able to take advantage of them.

When all is considered, most behaviorists agree that the hostility we bear toward others is likely a displacement of our own displeasure with life. A survey by *Psychology Today* found that those people who are generally grouchy are also most likely to be lonely, depressed, and suffer from low self-esteem. Indeed, the findings show that animosity is directly linked to poor emotional well-being.

Do You Live with Loneliness?

Loneliness is such a universal human condition, it has been called the common cold of psychopathology. But loneliness isn't just a matter of being alone. Many factors contribute to its impact. The fact is, loneliness is a widely misunderstood state of mind. A survey of 25,000 people by New York University (N.Y.U.) sociologists revealed some interesting findings on the subject. The overall conclusion of the study was that mistaken notions abound about man's oldest interpersonal problem.

TEST

How much do you know about loneliness? Take the following quiz, which explores a number of the findings of the N.Y.U. study, to find out.

1. If I live alone, I'm more prone to loneliness than if I live with someone.

True   False

2. If I had money, a good job, and plenty of education, I would be less vulnerable to feeling lonely.

True   False

3. Chances are that if I were an only child, I would be lonelier than someone who had brothers and sisters.

True   False

4. Generally, women are lonelier than men.

True   False

5. It's tough to make friends today because people are more into themselves than others.

True   False

6. Children of lonely parents also tend to be lonely.

True   False

7. Early separation from parents has no direct effect on the loneliness we may experience as adults.

True   False

8. Loneliness is an inborn, basic part of our personality and, as such, can't be changed much.

True   False

9. As a group, the elderly feel more lonely and isolated than those who are younger.

True   False

10. Lonely people usually have a poor image of themselves.

True   False

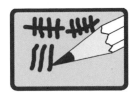

SCORING

To tally your score, give yourself 1 point for each response that matches yours.

1. *False.*   **2.** *True*   **3.** *False*   **4.** *False*   **5.** *False*   **6.** *True*   **7.** *False*
8. *False*   **9.** *False*   **10.** *True*

A score of 7 points or more: You have an adequate grasp of the causes of loneliness. You have the capacity to understand those who are lonely and to help yourself if loneliness strikes.

A score of 6 points or less: You have some false assumptions about loneliness. A low score doesn't necessarily mean that you are lonely, but suggests that you don't understand this most human of emotions.

EXPLANATION

To correct or confirm your hunches about loneliness, read on for detailed explanations of the items on the quiz.

1. *False.* Author Thomas Wolfe once described loneliness as a sure cure for vanity. It certainly can be a sobering experience. But not all solitary people feel lonely. A lot depends upon how they interpret their situation. A hermit, recluse, or explorer, for instance, may be isolated but may not suffer from it because he perceives his lot as something self-imposed and over which he has some control. On the other hand, a teenager in the midst of his classmates may, by contrast, feel sharply alone and rejected. He mistakenly feels he has no choice about changing his fate.

2. *True.* Money does count in combating loneliness. The survey found that the loneliest people were likely to be poor and uneducated. Simply put, money and education help to put us in the right places socially and offer us the opportunity to meet interesting people.

3. *False.* Only children have usually learned to adjust to being alone. Studies show that they are actually less apt to feel lonely than children with siblings.

4. *False.* Studies have found that men view loneliness as unmanly and are therefore less likely to admit to feeling it on most surveys. It is likely that men are lonelier than women, because women tend to communicate their feelings more readily and thus are able to receive support from others.

5. *False.* Letitia A. Peplau, an authority on loneliness, says that many loners blame their plight on the indifference of others. But it's much more likely that their isolation is due to their own shyness, fear of rejection, and lack of basic social skills.

6. *True.* Loners often report that their parents were also lonely. They describe them as disagreeable, remote, and uninvolved. Those who weren't lonely saw their parents as close, warm, and cheerful.

7. *False.* The N.Y.U. survey confirmed what many child psychologists have claimed, that parental separation can produce "separation anxiety" and have lasting effects on children. As adults, such people are prone to feeling lonely when apart from others.

8. *False.* No matter what your developmental circumstances were, a sense of loneliness can be overcome. Dr. Gerald Phillips, director of the Friendship Clinic at University Park in Pennsylvania, heads a staff that teaches social skills to those who wish to expand their social contacts. He says that loners must overcome a variety of attitudes about social insecurity, self-depreciation, and low self-esteem. If these personal hang-ups can be surmounted, then much of the loneliness that Americans suffer can be eliminated.

9. *False.* A large survey of the elderly conducted at Duke University in North Carolina found that about two-thirds of this group claimed that they are seldom or never lonely. Their contacts with relatives and friends in senior centers are more frequent than commonly believed.

10. *True.* Being isolated from society is most often a choice we make ourselves. It is strongly tied in with our perceptions of ourselves. At the heart of it is a "guiding fiction" that we are, or will be, unacceptable and disliked by others.

If you are among the lonely, you can help yourself. You need people in your life! Try finding others in your community who share your interests by joining a book group, gardening club, or historical society. Volunteer to work with those less fortunate than yourself. Chances are, you'll meet people and make friends who can take the edge off your loneliness. Remember, loneliness is by and large a choice: You can either accept it or overcome it.

Would You Resist Psychotherapy?

In the United States alone, an estimated 30 million people a year suffer some form of mental illness—and many of these people do not seek help. The millions who don't receive attention are often plagued by indecisiveness and hesitation about psychotherapy. Some reasons for this hesitation include a faulty understanding of just what the process entails. But most of the resistance comes from deeper attitudes associated with shame, fear, and the tarnished social image they feel will result from being a patient. These notions block many needy people from getting the care that can help them.

TEST

Would you enter therapy if you were told you needed it? More importantly, would you possess the attitudes necessary to benefit from it? To find out, take the following quiz, which is based on the work of psychologists E. Fischer and J. Le B. Turner.

1. I probably wouldn't vote for anyone who had struggled with an emotional problem in the past.

True False

2. Building a strong character is the best way to overcome mental illness.

True False

3. Like many other things, emotional difficulties tend to work themselves out.

True False

4. When getting help, the main caution is to avoid getting the wrong advice.

True False

5. Keeping my mind on a job is a good remedy for avoiding worries.

True False

6. Having been a psychiatric patient is a serious blot on a person's life.

True False

7. I would see a psychotherapist only after I'd tried for a long while to solve my own problems.

True False

8. It's probably best not to know everything about myself.

True False

9. Compared with my friends, I am a very closed person.

True False

10. People who go to a psychotherapist could have helped themselves if they had tried harder.

True False

SCORING

To tally your score, give yourself 1 point for each "True" response.

A score of 6 points of more: You're likely to be resistant to therapy. The closer your score is to 10, the more resistant you will be.

A score of 5 points or less: You would be open to receiving psychotherapy if necessary.

Research shows that women tend to be more accepting of psychotherapy than men. This probably has a lot to do with social conditioning—men usually try hard to live up to an image of independence, and tend not to ask someone else for help.

EXPLANATION

Read on for more detailed explanations of the items on the quiz.

1. *False.* Those who believe that an emotional crisis has lasting effects on one's judgment have difficulty believing that one can regain stability after an emotional upset. These people tend to make poor prospects for psychotherapy.

2. *False.* Character has little to do with mental health. Regrettably, those who think otherwise may someday suffer needlessly because of this attitude.

3. *False.* More often than not, a serious mental disturbance tends to worsen with time.

4. *False.* Poor advice can be detrimental, but a competent therapist will minimize the danger of this happening.

5. *False.* It is wishful thinking to believe that distractions, like a job or love affair, will lead to resolution of a personal crisis.

6. *False.* People with poor attitudes toward psychotherapy often use social stigma about mental illness as an excuse to avoid treatment.

7. *False.* Procrastinators often reflect fear or resistance about changing themselves. They usually break with therapy too soon to be helped.

8. *False.* People who aren't receptive to new insights into themselves don't benefit from treatment.

9. *False.* Studies confirm that those who feel comfortable in revealing themselves stand the best chance of benefiting from psychotherapy.

10. *False.* Trying harder to "cure" yourself isn't enough to solve fairly serious emotional problems. This notion merely provides the resistant person with yet another reason for staying away from therapy.

No matter how you scored on this quiz, keep in mind that if your motivation to be helped is high enough, your chances of solving your problems are greatly increased.

Can You Spot the Signs of Creeping Alcoholism?

The American Council on Alcoholism in Alexandria, Virginia, reports that 10 percent of the United States' population (some 20 million people) has a serious problem with alcohol. In addition to being a mental health problem, excessive drinking can also lead to or exacerbate physical ailments like diabetes, hypertension, and liver disease. If you've noticed changes in your drinking patterns lately, observe them carefully—you may be a candidate for addiction.

TEST

To find out if your drinking habits have the potential to turn into a problem, take the following quiz.

1. I'll have a drink before going to a gathering where I know liquor will be served.
True False

2. I drink when I'm feeling blue.
True False

3. I'll have a drink before and/or after a stressful event.
True False

4. I tend to drink more than my friends do.
True False

5. I'll have more than three drinks per day, even when alone.
True False

6. I occasionally tipple in the morning before going to work or school.
True False

7. I imbibe to steady my nerves.
True False

8. I gulp my alcoholic beverages.
True False

9. I feel it is necessary to have two or more drinks at certain times, like before lunch, at dinner, or after work.
True False

10. I have boozed to the point of feeling ill.
True False

SCORING

To tally your score, give yourself 1 point for each "True" response.

A score of 5 or more points: You may be developing a drinking problem. Take steps immediately to intervene before your drinking turns into an addiction. You might consider talking to a trusted friend or therapist.

A score of 4 points or less: Your drinking habits seem to be under control. If you think a friend or loved one would score high on this quiz, you might want to consider having a conversation with that person about his or her drinking.

EXPLANATION

Authorities at the Menninger Foundation for Psychiatry in Topeka, Kansas, believe that most alcoholics have undiagnosed mental disturbances and drink to quell or cover up these problems. In addition, alcoholics bear the distinction of profoundly affecting others in their family circle. Each alcoholic adversely affects about six people he knows, bringing the total number of people who can use alcohol-related support resources to 120 million.

Alcoholism costs the American economy some $50 billion annually, to say nothing of its toll in human suffering. Over-indulging is not restricted to the United States, either. The addiction can be found worldwide. Both France and Russia, for example, have declared that alcoholism is their number one public health concern.

The American grassroots organization MADD (Mothers Against Drunk Driving) has probably done more to publicize the abuse of alcohol within the past twenty-five years than any other civic group. Its campaigns are aimed primarily at teenagers who drink and drive. In this age group, liquor is far and away the main substance addiction, exceeding that of tobacco and drugs. The age group from seventeen to twenty-five consumes proportionately far more cigarettes, liquor, and drugs than that of any other age bracket. As a result, this group is the prime target for peddlers of such products.

How Self-Conscious Are You?

Of all living creatures, man is the only one who is self-conscious. This ability to reflect upon ourselves as an object can be used constructively to correct our faulty behavior. But, if carried to extremes, self-consciousness can be a hindrance.

Research done by Dr. P. A. Pilkonis while at Stanford University revealed two types of self-consciousness: private and public. Being privately self-conscious involves a feeling about yourself that is usually unfavorable, such as "I'm fat," "I'm lazy," or "I'm shallow." Public self-consciousness, on the other hand, reflects your sensitivity about how others will judge or think about you. In this age of style and image, where there is more emphasis on form than on substance, a common type of public self-consciousness is concern about one's appearance. Judging from the billions of dollars spent yearly on clothes and cosmetics, this is uppermost in the minds of many people.

TEST

To gauge your own level of public self-consciousness, take the following quiz.

1. I probably wouldn't sing solo at a party.
a. Disagree   *b.* Somewhat agree   *c.* Strongly agree

2. I would feel uneasy if someone watched me work.
a. Disagree   *b.* Somewhat agree   *c.* Strongly agree

3. It makes me feel "nervous" if a stranger nearby makes a fool of himself.
a. Disagree   *b.* Somewhat agree   *c.* Strongly agree

4. One of the last things I do before I go out is look in the mirror.
a. Disagree   *b.* Somewhat agree   *c.* Strongly agree

5. I would probably refuse to go up onto a stage if I were picked from an audience.
a. Disagree   *b.* Somewhat agree   *c.* Strongly agree

6. I would feel conspicuous if I were first to arrive or first to leave a small party of friends.
a. Disagree   *b.* Somewhat agree   *c.* Strongly agree

7. In public, I would feel conspicuous if I spent more than a few seconds in front of a mirror.
a. Disagree   *b.* Somewhat agree   *c.* Strongly agree

8. On a crowded bus, I would feel embarrassed if I offered my seat to someone who loudly declined it.
a. Disagree   *b.* Somewhat agree   *c.* Strongly agree

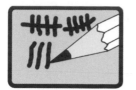

SCORING

To tally your score, give yourself 1 point for each "a" response, 2 points for each "b" response, and 3 points for each "c" response.

A score of 19–24 points: You possess a great deal of public self-consciousness. It's possible that you are too sensitive to what others think of you. You are also likely to be susceptible to feelings of rejection.

A score of 12–18 points: You have an average degree of public self-consciousness. You're aware of others' perceptions of you, but not to the point that it stifles your self-expression or shakes your self-confidence.

A score of 8–11 points: Your level of public self-consciousness is very low. People in this category may lack awareness of how they appear to others and/or may show too little concern for what people think of them.

EXPLANATION

Public or social self-consciousness starts in infancy. When a child faces a situation that challenges his self-image, like being criticized or scolded for being rude to others, it tends to heighten his concern about being judged negatively. Being raised by overly critical adults usually results in excessive public as well as private self-consciousness. This trait often leads to introversion.

But public self-consciousness isn't always as bad as it may seem. Some publicly self-conscious people have a good image of themselves and are not privately self-conscious at all. They can be loners who nevertheless engage in constructive pursuits. Well-known people who have been publicly self-conscious include Abraham Lincoln, Thomas Edison, and Ludwig van Beethoven.

However, extreme public self-consciousness can be practically immobilizing. Those who are constantly having self-reflective thoughts are often shy, socially insecure, and sensitive to criticism. They avoid competition. Often, they are charitable to almost everyone except themselves. Charlie Chaplin's vivid portrayal of the forlorn tramp exemplifies such a person. He tries hard to please everyone he meets. Like many who are painfully self-conscious, Chaplin's character is a lovable person with many fine qualities. The trouble is that he and others like him rarely believe in their own positive qualities.

Those who are very self-aware are often silent around others. But they can learn to become more assertive and outgoing. One study conducted at Stanford University showed that quiet people who are encouraged to speak while in a group can change the way the group perceives them. When the subjects were silent, group members tended to ignore or minimize their position in the group. But when they began to express ideas and opinions, others' attitudes changed. Many subjects went from exhibiting a strong degree of public self-consciousness and shyness to assuming a leadership position within the group.

Are You Bound for a Coronary?

One day an upholsterer who was repairing chairs in a doctors' reception room commented that the seats were worn out only on the front edges. This chance remark caused cardiologists Meyer Friedman and Ray Rosenman, at Mt. Zion Medical Center in San Francisco, to wonder about the traits of their cardiac patients—were they overly anxious and therefore leaning forward in their chairs, rubbing away the fabric? After several studies they found evidence that peoples' personalities did indeed affect their behavior, and as a natural result, their health. For the first time they isolated, defined, and named the specific behavior pattern closely associated with coronary heart disease, which they labeled "A-Type." Their subsequent book, *A-Type Behavior and Your Heart*, came to significantly influence the way we think about how our actions affect our heart.

TEST

The A-Type personality has a compulsive sense of urgency combined with an intensely competitive drive. B-Types, who are at the other end of the spectrum, tend to be calmer, more patient, and more adaptable (and consequently gentler on their hearts). To find out if your personality type might lead to some troubles with your ticker, take the following quiz.

1. I tend to do things rapidly, such as walking, eating, and getting dressed.
True   False

2. I find it satisfying to do many things at the spur of the moment and without much reflection.
True   False

3. I often have little time to have my hair cut or styled.
True   False

4. I frequently face interruptions and unexpected or last-minute changes.
True   False

5. I am impatient and sometimes even angry when someone ahead of me drives slowly.
True   False

6. I often do two or more things at once, such as reading while eating, typing while talking on the phone, or scanning a magazine while watching TV.
True   False

7. I hate to waste time.
True   False

8. I usually arrive just a few minutes before my train or plane is due to depart.
True   False

9. Compared to most of my friends, I lose my temper easily.
True   False

10. I am a competitive person.
True   False

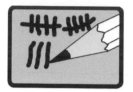

SCORING

To tally your score, give yourself 1 point for each "True" response.

A score of 8-10: Watch out heart—you tend towards being an A-Type.

A score of 4–7: You are about average, though you may exhibit A-Type behavior on occasion.

A score of 0-3: You are a B-Type personality, and relatively easygoing.

EXPLANATION

The A-Type is a stressed, often angry or frustrated individual. His compulsive sense of urgency, more graphically called "hurry sickness," compels him to achieve more in less time.

People who have A-Type personalities evaluate their merit by numeration. For example, if an A-Type were a lawyer, he or she might mention how many cases were handled in the past year; if he or she were a real-estate broker, how many houses were sold; if a gardener, how many lawns were mowed.

It must be said that most of the world's achievers are A-Types. According to Dr. Friedman's findings, they succeed despite their self-created stress. Still, there are some quietly achievement-minded individuals who exhibit B-Type behavior and get ahead. Some notable B-Types include Abraham Lincoln, Ronald Reagan, and Jimmy Carter.

On the physical level, A's have a tougher time with their coronary health. They tend to metabolize cholesterol more slowly than do B's, which gives them a greater propensity for clogged arteries. This seems to be a genetic factor, though B-Types have been known to adapt A-Type behavior (and symptoms) when under increased amounts of stress.

Although being an A-Type is a considerably riskier existence than being a B, there are ways that A's can train themselves to adopt B-Type characteristics. By learning to relax, eat healthfully, and set realistic life goals, many A-Types have successfully overcome their natural tendencies and protected themselves against further heart disease and damage.

Do You Sing Before Breakfast: How Happy Are You?

Happiness is a relative state of mind. Some of us would be content living in a cave, while others would be miserable in a mansion. Throughout the ages, philosophers have pondered the meaning of happiness. Is it a balance between need and satisfaction? A harmony between that which we desire and that which we receive? A baby? A sports car? However we define happiness, one thing is certain: We know it when we don't have it.

TEST

If you've ever wondered how you compare with others on the happiness scale, the following quiz might provide some answers.

1. I cease to enjoy a game when I am losing badly.

True **False**

2. I can enjoy a joke when it is on me.

True **False**

3. I am pleased when a friend receives praise in my presence.

True **False**

4. If a person cuts in front of me in a line, I always openly object to it.

True **False**

5. I get bored easily with hobbies.

True **False**

6. I daydream often.

True **False**

7. I wish for many things.

True **False**

8. I am overweight.

True **False**

9. I enjoy reading fiction.

True **False**

10. I hate to go to bed.

True **False**

11. I think I am attractive and/or personable.

True **False**

12. I take criticism well.

True **False**

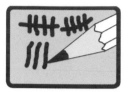

SCORING

To tally your score, give yourself 1 point for each correct answer.

1. *False*   **2.** *True*   **3.** *True*   **4.** *False*   **5.** *False*   **6.** *False*   **7.** *False*
8. *False*   **9.** *True*   **10.** *False*   **11.** *True*   **12.** *True*

A score of 9–12 points: Compared with others, you are quite a happy person. You seem to maintain a good balance between what you expect out of life and what you actually receive. High scorers like you are socially well-adjusted. You are attractive to others because of your live-and-let-live attitude.

A score of 5–8 points: You have your ups and downs but for the most part, you are moderately happy. There's no burning desire to change your life. You'd probably have an uplifting effect on someone who is less happy than you, but at the same time, you could benefit if you associated with those happier than yourself.

A score of 0–4 points: You could be much happier! Somehow, you've developed a perspective on life that is a bit lopsided. Review each of your answers and try to figure out how you can change your perspective.

EXPLANATION

This quiz is based on the work of the late Dr. Theo F. Lentz, former director of the Character Research Association in St. Louis, Missouri. He conducted the largest study ever done on the topic of happiness. Lentz's subjects were men and women ranging in age from sixteen to fifty years, with a minimum of twelve years of education. From the data collected, Lentz composed a "happiness scale." Read on for more detailed explanations of each quiz item.

1. *False.* A happy person can still like himself when he's losing because he believes he has other admirable qualities, and draws upon them to support a positive self-image.

2. *True.* Happy people are better able to laugh at themselves, because they have such a positive self-image to begin with. They don't take themselves too seriously.

3. *True.* A happy person can empathize with and praise others. He has enough good feelings about himself to take a backseat and not envy someone in the limelight.

4. *False.* A happy person can allow small indiscretions by others without feeling vindictive or deprived.

5. *False.* Compared with someone who is unhappy, a happy person has enough resiliency to sustain effort in an activity. He doesn't discourage easily. He can tolerate periods of frustration and boredom on his way to a distant goal.

6. *False.* A happy person does not compensate for an unhappy frame of mind by wishful thinking and daydreaming.

7. *False.* Happy people tend not to wish for many things, because they already feel content with what they have.

8. *False.* If you're happy, you probably don't overindulge. Overeaters are usually unhappy and try to gain, through sense pleasures, the satisfactions they don't receive in other ways.

9. *True.* Happy people don't feel compelled to stick with factual material. They like fiction. They are flexible enough to depart from reality and enjoy someone else's imagination.

10. *False.* It's not clear why, but compared with those who are unhappy, people who are content don't find it difficult to go to bed. Perhaps the unhappy find it hard to end the day because they've had few pleasurable moments and as a result, push themselves beyond bedtime, hoping that a moment of satisfaction will occur.

11. *True.* If you're happy, you are generally accepting and not condemning of yourself. Unhappy folks often have a poor body image and harbor many self-critical thoughts.

12. *True.* Happy people don't feel diminished when their faults are exposed and can take criticism without being defensive.